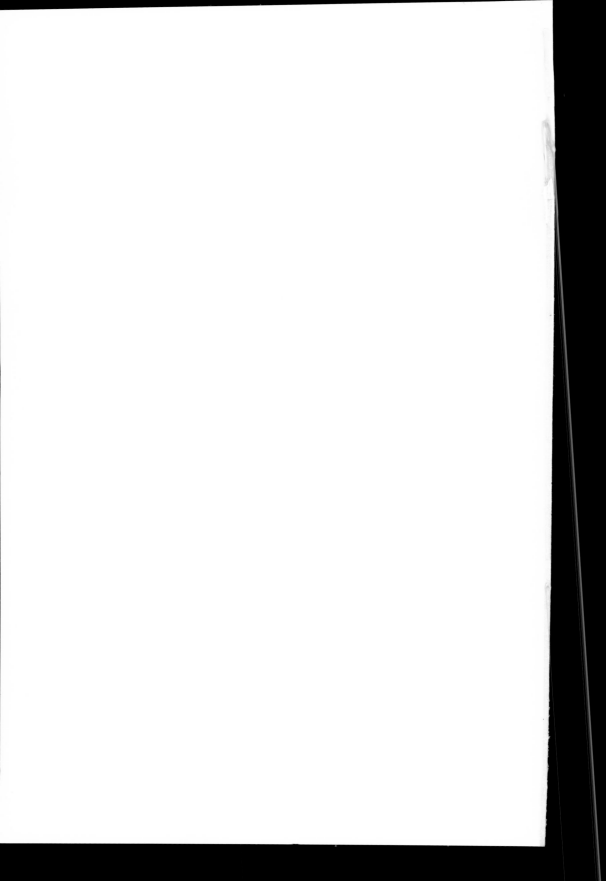

Rude Awakening

Dear Brad and Barbra ~
Your belief in me and your
avid support of this
Project mean so much to me.
Many, many thanks.
With love,
Sheree Ann Martines

SHEREE ANN MARTINES
WITH JOHN ROBERT WHEDBEE

PAGE PUBLISHING, INC.
Conneaut Lake, PA

First originally published by Page Publishing 2019

ISBN 978-1-64462-032-8 (pbk)
ISBN 978-1-64584-973-5 (hc)
ISBN 978-1-64462-033-5 (digital)

Printed in the United States of America

FOREWORD

I would like to take this foreword as an opportunity to make my reasons known for telling this story now, after so many years. I intend for this book to set the record straight and maybe achieve some degree of vindication for myself. At the time in my life when these events were occurring, I followed the advice of attorneys who had instructed me to be quiet, to not talk to the media, and consequently, I did not have the opportunity to tell the whole story, the way it really happened. It is my opinion that the story provided to the public was a tale crafted by defense attorneys, who put a spin on the facts pursuing an acquittal for their client and reporters who were concerned with successfully selling a marketable tale rather than providing access to the truth.

My hope is that my story will inspire others who have been victims of violent crime at the hands of their spouse or other trusted person, who have undoubtedly seen their families torn apart, to pick themselves up and move forward in rebuilding their lives. I want those same people who have experienced this atrocious form of betrayal as well as, like in my case, the betrayal of our ultimately flawed legal system to know that it is possible to live, achieve, and maybe even trust again.

The operations of our legal and criminal justice systems are another item I would like to bring to light through this book. I suspect that many people do not fully understand that the scales of justice are not always as balanced as we would like to think. The prosecution is only able to present information that can be supported with evidence, whereas the defense may put forth theories and make accusations without presenting a shred of evidentiary support. This lesson was a painful one for me to learn as I watched the defense attorney put forth a case for the defendant that was largely fabricated and required no support, casting doubt on the prosecution's evidence and, furthermore, me as the victim. I was shocked and dismayed that the defense could so easily vilify me in the effort to acquit my own would-be murderers. Before this, I perceived the justice system to be about determining the truth, punishing the guilty, and delivering justice on behalf of the innocent. Unfortunately, I believed incorrectly, as many people continue to do. I found out the hard way that the idea of a fair justice system is not true, by a long shot. Hopefully, this book will serve its purpose and enlighten at least some portion of this number.

I would also like to take this opportunity to give credit to and show my utmost appreciation for my parents who gladly and unselfishly spent much of their time and energy to help me raise my children. Being a single parent is a situation that the word *difficult* does not even begin to describe for both the parent and the children. Our lives as they are today would not have been possible without their help; they gladly stepped up to try to alleviate the pressure on me as well as try to help soothe the pain of my children's abandonment on the part of their mother. I know how lucky I was, and am, to have this kind of support.

I furthermore hope to take this opportunity to offset some of the financial toll I have suffered due to the events that occurred during this part of my life. Any funds earned from the telling of my story will be used to improve not only my life but also the lives of my children, one of whom will require around-the-clock care for the rest of her life due to her many significant handicaps.

Newspapers and television networks have ultimately profited by telling their perception of my story for more than two decades, without much concern for the truth of the matter. I have watched my good name denigrated in the headlines, causing irreparable damage to my reputation. It is not feasible to expect a jury to unhear a testimony on command. I can only hope that this endeavor can help bring the truth to light once and for all, and maybe help someone experiencing multi-layered betrayal, benefit from the retelling of my story.

John Robert Whedbee

CHAPTER 1

The last hints of spring were fading away on that cool June night. The sharp, crescent sliver of the moon glowed a bright silver, illuminating the black canvas of the night sky. In the early morning hours, most of Knoxville, Tennessee, was peaceful and quiet, asleep, and unaware of the murderous threat lurking in the nice, quiet enclave of Camelot subdivision.

He was crouched like a rat in a hole, stiff from the six hours he had lain in wait in the cramped confines of the basement closet. The tall, wiry man was dying for a cigarette and began to contemplate, creeping outside for another one; he smoked compulsively, and the craving for a Virginia Slim was winning out over his resolve. Cautiously, he eased open the closet door and listened: the house was silent and still. He stealthy crept out like a thief in the night through the sliding glass door. The flame sliced through the dark for a second as he lit up and took a long drag.

He was pleased with himself, even proud, as he anticipated his role in a grand plan that had been months in the making. He had meticulously selected his garb: black jeans, socks, shoes, and even his black *Phantom of the Opera* T-shirt, as a way of solidifying his idea of himself as romantic hero. He wore a pair of latex gloves and kept a black stocking mask, which he would don later, crammed into one of his pockets.

He snubbed out his smoke, tossed the butt out into the yard, made the short trek back to his berth. He was infused with adrenaline as he envisioned his mission. He was there to slay the dragon and rescue the woman who he loved, driven on by his consuming desire for her. He would save her, and she would be his! *She would be his at last!* His heart thundered as he clutched the wicked blade and waited for her word. Michael Frazier, preacher's son and choir boy, was about to commit cold-blooded murder.

CHAPTER 2

Rising in the westward shadows of the Great Smoky Mountains and situated at the head of the Tennessee River, Knoxville, the third largest city in Tennessee, adorns the horizon. Its proximity to the rolling hills and mountain peaks of the Smokies, its abundance of lakes and rivers, and its mild climate make it an ideal venue for those seeking outdoor beauty and adventure. Rich in Appalachian culture and historical legends, locals are proud of their heritage.

Driven by a strong economy, infused with the vitality of a college town, Knoxville offers a colorful tapestry of opportunities and entertainment. While affording the amenities of the big cities, most natives will tell you Knoxville still possesses a certain small town charm. Much of the old architecture has been preserved and nicely blends with the new.

The University of Tennessee's beginning dates to 1794. Originally established as Blount College, the school went on to become the main campus of the University of Tennessee. Today, UT is recognized as the largest research institute in Tennessee, offering more than three hundred degree programs to its student census of approximately twenty-eight thousand. UT is especially respected for its agriculture and engineering programs and is home to the Tennessee Volunteers. Knoxvillians take their football and their beloved "Vols," as the locals say, with a religious fervor. On game days, rivers of orange flow through town as students and residents turn out to support their team.

About twenty-five miles west of Knoxville sits Oak Ridge, an area once shrouded in secrecy. Chosen by the United States Federal

Government in 1942 to be the research facility for the Manhattan Project, the government felt that the location's accessibility by highway and rail and readily available water and electricity resources, along with its situation within a long valley between two ridges, made it an ideal facility for the secret development of the atomic bomb. During the war, more than seventy thousand people were brought in to work on the top secret project.

In 1982, Knoxville opened its doors to the world, drawing more than eleven million visitors to the World's Fair. President Ronald Reagan spoke at the opening of the fair, which is deemed one of the most successful World's Fairs in history. Its theme "Energy Turns the World" underscored Knoxville's technological prominence. The Sunsphere, built for the fair, still glitters along the city skyline.

The diversity and quality of life that Knoxville offers seem to rank highest with most folks. Most residents, if asked, would say that it is an idyllic place to live and raise a family.

CHAPTER 3

John Robert Whedbee was born in Knoxville on November 25, 1960. It was the start of a new decade: John F. Kennedy and Lyndon B. Johnson had just won the presidency, *To Kill a Mockingbird* had just hit the shelves at bookstores, and US troops were headed to Vietnam.

Rob was the second son of Lloyd and Joyce Whedbee. He grew up in a happy home with loving parents who taught their sons strong values, respect for others, and the importance of working hard for what they wanted. The boys also learned the importance of the truth. Honesty was always the rule. The parents also passed on to their sons the meaning of family. Through good times and bad, family was the cornerstone. Together, they celebrated the bright moments and pulled together with strength and support during darker days.

For Rob Whedbee, childhood was jam-packed with happy memories. He learned to fish around the age of six, a pastime he would enjoy all his life. Living in a house on Kantebury Drive, he frequently walked the two blocks around the corner to visit with Pappy Garfield and Nanny Hazel, his grandparents on Carson Avenue. Sometimes during the summer and after school, he and his buddies would rough and tumble on the big rocks at the park down the street. There was swimming and tubing in Little River near his grandparents' cabin in Townsend. There was bike riding, skateboarding, and many a ball game to fill a kid's need for fun and activity. Rob often said his life was sort of like a Norman Rockwell painting. He was a good kid living a good life.

When Rob was nine, his family moved to Lakemoor Hills in south Knoxville. It was a big rambling house just off Lake Loudoun, and there were always a million ways to entertain growing boys. It was there he met his best friend, Hugh Ladd, and the two were almost always together brewing up some way to enjoy the day. Rob and Hugh would remain lifelong friends.

The two wandered the neighborhood and surrounding areas, playing on the playground, shooting hoops at the Presbyterian Church, boating on the lake, and enjoying lots of swimming and waterskiing. As they entered their teens, chasing girls became another activity of interest.

Rob had become well aware of girls in his early teens. Quite handsome, with a great personality, athletic build, and sense of humor, Rob had his share of girls who showed interest in him. His mother had brought him up to be a gentleman, and he made a point to always treat girls with respect and courtesy.

When Rob was fifteen, he fell in love, and he fell hard. While vacationing with his parents in Destin, Florida, he met a beautiful girl named Suzonne. It was not *just* a fling but a relationship that would endure through the years.

Suzonne lived in Louisiana, but that didn't slow Rob down. Shortly after his return to Knoxville, he was determined to track her down. And of course, when Rob set his mind to something it wasn't *if*, it was *when*. After reaching her on the phone, their relationship was on. With their parents' approval and supervision, Rob and Suzonne talked every Sunday. Over the next few years, they periodically met in Louisiana or Knoxville.

Although they never talked about an exclusive relationship, and Rob did date other girls in high school, in the back of his mind, he believed Suzonne would be the girl he would marry. However, with 612 miles between them and the infrequent visits, distance began to take its toll in the third year of their relationship.

After many discussions, they concluded that maybe the relationship wasn't meant to be and maybe their love had run its course. They were just kids when it started, and now they were each on the brink of adulthood with its ensuing responsibilities.

Rob was sad, and Suzonne was heartbroken, but when they agreed to stay friends, it was not just careless talk. They both meant it, and their paths would cross many times over the years.

Always athletic, Rob actively pursued and excelled in school sports. His mom said he was always playing something—football, basketball, and baseball—only his uniform changed with the seasons. He remained active in the big three sports throughout high school and became interested in boxing and powerlifting through some of the local clubs. After high school, Rob continued to box and compete in powerlifting events, traveling to Chicago; Dothan, Alabama; and Chattanooga and other locations around the country for tournaments.

During high school, Rob began to work at his family's insurance agency as a policy rater. He also conducted property inspections using a Polaroid camera, something that has mostly been replaced in the digital era.

At eighteen, Rob passed his insurance licensing exam; and in addition to going to UT full-time, he also invested as many hours as he could working at his parents' agency. The agency was still in its infancy stage, and Rob played a pivotal role in helping grow the business. He was smart, was a hard worker, and had excellent people skills; and at nineteen, he was already starting to make a decent living in the industry.

CHAPTER 4

Although Rob Whedbee worked hard at the agency, he was still a teenager and made time to hang out with friends, checking out the lively weekend activity that hummed around the streets and joints near UT.

Good-looking, athletic, and an ambitious young man, Rob often caught the eye of the girls out for a fun night. So when he and his buddy, Rick, tooled down Kingston Pike in Rob's black T-top Corvette one night, it was no surprise to see two girls in a blue Triumph TR6, flagging them down, telling them to pull over into the Copper Cellar parking lot. A blonde bounced out of the passenger seat, and Rob clearly heard her say to her friend, "I get the driver."

She was attractive, slim, *and* nicely endowed. Rob had no problem seating her beside him in his Corvette. Rick, obligingly, took his place in the Triumph, next to her friend, a pretty redhead.

Pulling back on to Kingston Pike, they made the turn at Cumberland Avenue and continued to cruise the strip. In Rob's Vette, the couple made small talk. She was a senior at Bearden High School where she ran track. Rob told her he was a sophomore at UT and worked in his family's insurance agency.

The conversation rattled on in a superficial manner as they learned bits and pieces about the other. She showed him where she lived, and they stopped at Sam and Andy's to get a bite—just an innocent outing between two teens.

It was getting late when they met back up with their friends— time to call it a night. The blonde pulled out a piece of paper from her purse and wrote down her number. She handed it to him and said, with her sweet smile, "Please call me."

Her name was Lisa Outlaw.

CHAPTER 5

Lisa Outlaw was born in west Knoxville in December of 1962, the only daughter of Jo and Bill Outlaw. Growing up with rowdy brothers, Lisa was a princess in the eyes of her dad. Her relationship with her mother was another story.

Through middle and high school, Lisa suffered all the trials of teenage angst—shyness, acne, braces, and limp hair. She was described by classmates as quiet and somewhat of a loner, except for her constant shadow, a girl named Tammy. Following Lisa around like a puppy, Tammy seemed to idolize her, and their friendship would last long beyond high school. Tammy would do just about anything to win Lisa's approval, and that would be clearly seen in the years to come.

When Lisa became involved with the girls' track team at Bearden High, she seemed to come out of her shell a bit. Running track had given her a lithe figure while still leaving her with ample breasts. Some described her as being very pale with hard facial features accentuated by the heavy black eyeliner and makeup she wore. One friend commented that in the best light, Lisa was attractive, not beautiful but attractive. As she began to cross the line into adulthood, she would begin to show off her features in a more positive way, trying new ways to dress, apply makeup, and fix her hair. She became quite pretty. Lisa often spoke in a soft voice, and her demeanor seemed to be sweet. Sometimes, she truly was. Later, these traits would become a veneer she would hide behind—*sweet Lisa*.

Her family life was often the subject of Lisa's conversations. She often spoke of the abuse she had suffered at her mother's hands.

According to Lisa, she had once been severely beaten by her mother for pulling out a kitchen drawer so far that the silverware tumbled upon the floor. She also recounted how her mother, in anger, had pushed her down the stairs, leaving her with severe bruising. *These stories were probably a precursor of things to come.*

CHAPTER 6

It was a Wednesday afternoon, and Rob was looking for a note he had made regarding an upcoming powerlifting tournament. He came across a small slip of folded paper and was about to trash it when he remembered it was the phone number for that hot blonde.

He stared at it for several moments. He and Suzonne had only recently decided to go in different directions. He still adored her, but maybe it was time to stick his toe back in the water. He picked up the phone and dialed the number.

Lisa was elated to hear from him and quickly agreed to a date on Friday night. Not much of a small talker, Rob said, "Great. I'll pick you up around seven thirty. We can catch a movie or maybe get something to eat."

At nineteen, Rob lived a busy life, going to UT full-time and working at the family agency as much as he could, and he was still actively involved in competitive powerlifting. A date with a new girl might be just what he needed to spice up his life a bit.

Lisa seemed nervous but happy to see his black Corvette pull in her driveway. Rob opened her door, then came around, and got into the driver's side.

"So what do you want to do?" he asked.

"Why don't we catch a bite somewhere so we can get better acquainted," she suggested.

"Good idea. Is Sam and Andy's good for you?"

"Perfect," she said, flashing her best smile at him.

The date went well. They laughed and talked. She showed interest in his powerlifting and wanted to know more about what he did at his parents' agency. She seemed to skim over questions about her family but told him about track and how much she enjoyed it. She told him she hadn't decided what to do after she graduated that May. She wasn't sure she was cut out for college.

When it was time to go, Rob took her arm and guided her to the door. Lisa was glowing.

When they arrived at Lisa's front porch, before Rob could say a word, she pressed her body close to his and gave him a passionate kiss. Of course, Rob was excited. He was a nineteen-year-old guy, and he could feel her breasts rubbing against him. They stood there under the porch light making out until Lisa finally pulled away.

A little out of breath, she told him she had had a wonderful time and that she would really like to see him again. Aroused, Rob agreed and promised to call her sometime that week. Lisa was already totally infatuated. She remembered that her mother always told her she should marry a rich man. Lisa thought Mr. Rob Whedbee just might fit the bill. And so began the courtship of Rob Whedbee and Lisa Outlaw.

As spring took a solid foothold in Knoxville, the mountain laurel, wisteria, and azaleas painted the landscape with vivid color. Rob and Lisa had been dating for almost two months and, for the most part, had settled into an exclusive relationship.

Rob would try to get to her track meets occasionally, and Lisa would occasionally travel with him to some of his powerlifting events. They were getting along well and enjoying each other's company. They frequently double-dated with one of Lisa's girlfriends and her boyfriend, Joe Anderson. Joe was tall and lean—a nice-looking fellow with an easygoing personality. He and Rob hit it off famously and built a strong friendship they would share over the years.

As Rob and Lisa got closer, she became more open about her life and her family. She told Rob she had been seriously ill numerous times and had ended up in the emergency room and was hospitalized, although doctors had failed to determine what was wrong with her. She also talked about the discord with her mother, sharing some about the abuse she had suffered. She divulged a secret from the Outlaw household, telling him about the time her brother had attacked their father with a butcher knife. She would later show him the marks left on the door from this incident.

Rob could not believe it. There seemed to be a lot of "dys" in the function of the Outlaw family. Listening to her, Rob had a hard time fathoming what he was hearing. He had grown up in a harmonious home, and Lisa's sounded anything but. It concerned him a bit, but things were going smoothly between them, and his apprehensions slipped away.

Lisa's parents seemed to approve of her new boyfriend. Rob especially liked her father, Bill, who was a straightforward guy and always seemed sincerely interested in what was going on in Rob's life.

Rob's parents had always been welcoming of the friends he had brought home over the years, and they treated Lisa no differently. Rob did sense that perhaps Lisa might not have been their first choice for him. Had Joyce Whedbee been truthful, she would have told Rob she believed Lisa to be shallow and superficial, but she bit her tongue for Rob's sake, hoping the attraction would fade in time.

Things were rolling along smoothly in their relationship until Rob got word that Suzonne was coming to visit for a week. Not wanting to lie to Lisa or hide it from her, he told her about it one night when he was taking her home. He was ill-prepared for her reaction.

"What?" she screeched. "You're kidding me, right?"

Her voice began to get louder and louder as she slammed him with sarcasm.

"You asshole!" she screamed. Then she started crying. "I suppose you're just going to dump me for her."

Rob had never seen an adult throw a temper tantrum of that magnitude until that moment. It was downright scary. As with most men, he detested drama and had little patience with her outburst.

Hysterical, Lisa continued to cry and shriek, "How could you do something like this to me? I've done everything for you, and you're just going to sleep with *her*?"

She continued berating him, releasing a string of expletives like none he had ever experienced from anyone.

Rob tried to reassure her that it was just a visit between two old friends, but Lisa didn't seem to buy it. When Rob pulled up at her house, Lisa screamed loud enough for the entire neighborhood to hear, "I hate you!" Then she jumped out of the car and ran into the house before he could even stop the car.

Damn, thought Rob. *Crazy woman!* He just could not tolerate that kind of nonsense.

Suzonne came to town, prettier than ever and just as sweet as she had always been. They easily fell back into their close relationship during her visit. The only flaws in the week were the numerous, desperate calls from Lisa begging Rob to take her back.

After Suzonne left, Rob had some deep soul-searching to do. He had a lot of doubts about starting things up again with Lisa. He had never liked drama or hysterics, and he thought it might be best to take a step back from the relationship. He just wasn't sure what to do.

Saturday morning, as Rob was helping his dad in the yard, Joyce hollered out that Rob had a phone call. Joe Anderson was on the phone.

"Hey, Joe. What's going on?"

"Rob, I don't like to get into other people's business, but I think you need to go see Lisa. Keri[1] just called me and told me Lisa cut her wrists last night."

"God, Joe, are you kidding me? Is she in the hospital?"

"I think she's at home, Rob, but I think you should go talk to her."

"Why on earth would she do something like that?" Rob asked. "I have thought for a while she might have some problems. I guess I'll go see her. Thanks, Joe."

Rob hung up the phone and stood there in the kitchen for a few moments, shaking his head. Nothing in his life had prepared him for something like this. He was completely out of his element and didn't have a clue what to do, but he changed his clothes and drove over to her house anyway.

---

[1] The name has been changed to protect the anonymity of the person.

Jo Outlaw answered the door and said, in a cheery manner, "Hello, Rob. I'll get Lisa."

That wasn't really what he expected. He thought there would be a somber tone around the house. *Surely, they knew what Lisa had done.*

When Lisa appeared, she looked distraught. Her wrists did not seem to be bandaged, and before he could say anything, she asked, "Can we go someplace? Any place away from here?"

Rob opened the front door and said, "Let's go. We can ride over to the track and walk. It's a nice day."

The ride to the track was a quiet one. Rob didn't know what to say, and Lisa remained silent. The park was beautiful. Bradford pears were in full bloom, and every breeze freed some of the white flowers cloaking the trees. It looked like snow drifting to the ground.

When they were situated on a bench under a sycamore tree, Rob asked, "Okay. Let me see."

She turned over her arms, each wrist bearing tiny red scratch marks as if she'd used a safety razor or a plastic picnic knife. It certainly didn't look like she had made a serious attempt to take her life.

He asked, "What's going on, Lisa?"

Right on cue, Lisa began to cry and said, "My parents just don't understand me, and they don't treat me right. I just can't live in that house with all the turmoil. If I try to talk to my mom, she only ridicules me. On top of that, I didn't think I'd ever see you again, and I just didn't want to go on living. I love you, Rob, and when I'm with you, I feel safe. I don't worry about the problems at home."

"Promise me this will never happen again, Lisa," he said.

"It will *never* happen again. Just hold me and tell me everything will be all right."

Rob took her in his arms, but instead of relief, he was feeling a sense of dread.

Later that evening when he told his dad about it, Lloyd thought for a few moments and said, "Well, it's none of my business, but I'd think twice about continuing to see her. She's obviously got some problems, and if you keep dating her, they will become your problems too."

Despite his father's advice and his own misgivings, Rob decided to keep seeing her, spending even more time with her than before, but they rarely spent any time at her house. They went to the Smoky Mountains and to Rob's parents' place in Destin. They hung out with Joe Anderson and his girl. Everything seemed to be going well, and two years passed by in a flash.

CHAPTER 7

As 1981 rolled around, Rob had already turned twenty-one and was working hard to help build his family's company. He had left UT to work full-time as an agent, and business was going well. Lisa, now nineteen, had started helping around the Whedbees' office. She was a quick learner and had strong organizational skills. Rob was pleased with the work she did.

That was the year they started talking about moving in together. Their conversations always led to Lisa being adamant about getting married first, but Rob stood firm. He was in no way ready to make that commitment. He always told her they needed to wait.

One February afternoon, Rob received a frantic call from Lisa, telling him she needed to see him right away.

What now? he thought as he drove down Middlebrook Pike toward her house.

Lisa was waiting for him when he arrived. She led him to the living room and closed the doors so they could talk in private. She looked shaken up, and Rob wondered what was wrong. Finally, after they were both seated on the couch, she spoke.

"I'm pregnant," she said, her voice small and quiet.

Rob suddenly felt ill. This was the last thing he expected or wanted to hear. *Pregnant?*

"Are you sure?" he asked.

"Yes, I'm three weeks late."

At another time in his life, Rob would have been delighted to know he was going to be a father; but for now, the timing was all wrong. He did care for Lisa, but he still had concerns about her stability. Time stopped as he sat there, speechless, for several minutes. Lisa watched him, looking for some reaction.

At last, he spoke. "I've got to think about this, Lisa. I'll give you a call later."

"Are you upset with me?" she asked.

"No, I just need to think this thing through. Like I said, I'll call you later."

Driving back to the office, Rob felt a gnawing sensation in his chest. He wasn't ready for this, and neither set of parents was going to be happy he had gotten Lisa pregnant. He just didn't see any options. The right thing to do was to marry her, ready or not.

Sleep was elusive for Rob that night. He tossed and turned, wrestling with his problem, but in the morning light, he knew there was only one thing he could do.

He rose that morning and found his parents seated at the kitchen table. His dad was reading the *Knoxville News Sentinel,* and his mom was watching the morning news. Sausage and eggs she had made for him were on the range. Rob poured some orange juice and brought his plate over to the table. He ate several bites and then put down his fork.

"I need to tell you something."

Lloyd folded the paper, and Joyce muted the TV, waiting for Rob to speak.

"I've decided to marry Lisa."

They sat there in silence around the kitchen table. Joyce looked at Lloyd, and Lloyd looked back at her. Neither knew what to say. Lloyd finally spoke.

"Why so sudden? And with everything you've been through with this relationship, are you really sure you're ready to take this kind of step? I know you are a man, Rob, but you are young, and you've got plenty of time to find the right person."

Joyce chimed in on Lloyd's heels, "Rob, I really think you should reconsider. Lisa's a nice girl, but this just doesn't feel right."

Rob smiled at both of his parents and said, "I understand how you feel, but Ma and Pop, it will be okay."

Putting their reservations aside, they both wished him well, keeping any further doubts to themselves.

After talking with his parents, Rob knew what he had to do next. It may have seemed somewhat old-fashioned, but Rob intended to ask Lisa's father for her hand in marriage.

Pulling up in front of the Outlaw house, Rob saw Bill tinkering around in the garage. Lisa's family was much different than his own, but Bill Outlaw was a good and honest man, and he and Rob had always gotten along well.

Bill came from a small, rural area in Alabama. They didn't have much growing up, but they got by. Bill left Alabama behind and moved to Knoxville to work for the TVA as an engineering tech. He had worked hard over the years to provide for his family. A quiet man who usually kept his thoughts to himself, Bill Outlaw was a solid man who was always ready to help when needed.

"Howdy, Rob. How's it going? I think Lisa went shopping with a friend."

"Doing pretty good, Bill, but I actually came to speak with you," he said.

"Oh?" Bill replied, a little surprised. "Well, come on in, and we can talk."

The two stood there in silence for a few minutes until Rob finally blurted it out.

"Bill, I'd like your permission to marry your daughter."

There it was, out on the table. Bill picked up a rag and wiped the grease from his hands, using that time to reflect on Rob's request. When Bill finally spoke, Rob could not believe the words that came from his mouth.

"Rob, I don't think Lisa could do any better than a man like you, but…"

He paused for a moment, thoughtfully.

"Are you sure this is really what you want to do?"

Rob wondered what did Bill knew that he didn't.

"Yes, sir. I've made up my mind."

Bill patted him on the shoulder and said, "Well, if that's what you want, I'd be proud to have you as a son-in-law."

He reached out to shake Rob's hand.

"Maybe you can settle down that wild daughter of mine."

Rob and Bill spoke for a few more minutes before they said goodbye and parted ways. As he drove away, he thought perhaps he had misinterpreted what Bill was saying. It sure sounded as if he was trying to talk Rob out of marrying his own daughter. He had to admit he felt a bit worried, but the deed was done, and there was no turning back. He did not know his feelings of worry were only going to get worse.

Rob headed over to West Town Mall to buy an engagement ring before he changed his mind. Lisa would get a diamond, and he would get the proverbial ball and chain.

CHAPTER 8

Rob lay on his bed with his arms behind his head, looking up at the ceiling, thinking about that little black box on his dresser that seemed to define his future. Funny how a chip of diamond set in gold could be such a life changer.

It had been two days since he bought the ring. He had planned to propose every day, but deep in his heart, he was still praying some other option might surface. Red flags had been running rampant in their relationship so far—her phantom illnesses, her annoying neediness, her tendency toward hysteria, her half-hearted attempts at suicide, and of course, her own father's warning to Rob when he had asked for Lisa's hand in marriage. He wondered if getting married and starting a family would stabilize her behavior. It was what she had been begging for. He never imagined, that in time, it would make things worse.

Rob had always hoped he would find a relationship like his parents. They shared a caring partnership, working side by side, and treated each other with love and respect. He had grown up in a happy home where family was the most important thing. He knew he was lucky, *but now?*

In fairness, Rob had to admit Lisa was not without her charms. She was a good-looking girl who adorned his arm nicely. She had been supportive of Rob as he pursued his career and always tried to pump up his self-esteem. He hated to admit it, but she also put out, and guys his age, who weren't always thinking with their heads, liked that. Of course, that was what had gotten him in the mess he now faced.

Rob also had a relatively clear picture of Lisa's less-admirable qualities. Lisa was a master manipulator. She knew how to push people's buttons to get what she wanted. Rob had commented to his friend Hugh Ladd that Lisa was a bit like an orphan who wanted you to feel sorry for her because both of her parents were dead, and then you discovered that she killed both of them. She knew when she told him she was pregnant he would never turn his back on his responsibility.

So Friday night rolled around. Rob pocketed the little box, armed himself with a positive attitude, and drove to the Outlaw house. Lisa met him at the door, all bubbly and happy to see him. She gleefully threw her arms around him and then pulled him into the house.

"So," she asked, "what do you want to do tonight?"

Rob figured it was now or never, replying, "Why don't we go sit down and talk about it?"

"Sure," she said as they walked into the living room. "What's up?"

They sat on the couch, and Lisa pulled him toward her and kissed him. Rob had thought of a few ways to "pop the question," but he wasn't feeling especially romantic or sentimental, especially under the circumstances.

Finally, he pulled out the little box and handed it to her.

"I thought this might be something you would like."

Even before she opened it, she jumped in excitement.

"Really, Rob? Really?"

She slowly opened the box and began to scream, "Yes! Yes! Yes!"

Rob had never seen her so excited.

"We're going to get married? Really, Rob?" she asked again.

"Looks that way," Rob said.

Lisa put the ring on her finger and started flashing her hand around. She then went running down the hall to find her parents.

"Rob asked me to marry him!" she excitedly told her mom, showing off the ring on her finger.

Jo, Lisa's mom, was almost as ecstatic as Lisa. Her father reached out and shook Rob's hand heartily, saying, "Congratulations and welcome to the family."

No one could really know what Rob was feeling. He was doing his best to keep a smile plastered across his face, hoping to disguise his feelings of doubt.

"Rob, we've got to go tell your parents," Lisa stated emphatically. "Let's go right now!"

"Okay, okay," Rob said, nodding.

He was not looking forward to sharing the news with Joyce and Lloyd, knowing how they both felt. He was also worried about how disappointed they would be when they found out why he was marrying her.

On the way to his folk's house, Lisa insisted on stopping at the drugstore where she proceeded to buy every bridal magazine on the rack.

Oh boy, Rob thought.

When they broke the news to his parents, they acted appropriately surprised and happy, regardless of what they may have been thinking. God, he hated to let them down.

Over the next several days, the word got out. Lisa almost levitated in elation as she told all her friends and began to make plans. Rob, on the other hand, still felt weighed down with doubt about his decision.

Lisa was on fire and savored every moment of planning her wedding. She'd been dreaming about it since she was a small girl, and it was finally going to happen. Her dream had come true. She was marrying a gorgeous man who was stable and was on the way to making a very good living. She knew Rob would take good care of her, and finally, she would be able to have and do all the things that had been out of reach as she was growing up. Her mother had always told her to marry a rich man, and although Rob wasn't rich yet, *he would be*; she just knew it.

Immersed in wedding dresses, picking bridesmaids, and finding a photographer and a caterer, Lisa was in her element. Rob noticed she seemed much more stable and, therefore, much more appealing.

He began to feel a little better about things and even had her help him pick out tuxes.

Rob and Lisa did not discuss her pregnancy much. He really didn't like to talk about it, although he knew that in time, decisions would need to be made regarding the child on the way. So Rob was caught completely off guard when Lisa just casually mentioned, one April afternoon, that she wasn't pregnant. It had just been a mistake. Rob was so relieved. He really didn't think about it much, but as the years passed by, he would come to believe that she had never been pregnant, nor had she ever thought she was. He felt as if he had just been blindly outmaneuvered by another one of her deceptions. Lisa wasn't the smartest girl on the block, but she was crafty like a fox.

On the dawning of the wedding day, Rob awoke early. He had had a restless night, only sleeping intermittently. For the past several weeks, he had had a gnawing sensation in the pit of his stomach; and although most would say it was just prewedding jitters, he knew it was more than that. During those weeks, he had put on the face of a man happy about his future, but he knew the truth. Still he went through the motions, unsure how he would get through this day that would change his life forever.

Joe Anderson was already at the church when Rob arrived. By this time, Rob was seized with major anxiety, and Joe tried to joke with him to lighten the somberness that followed Rob around like a shadow. Rob was pacing like a caged tiger when he finally confided in Joe.

"Joe, I just don't think I can do this. It just doesn't feel right."

"Oh, you've just got a case of cold feet. You'll be fine. Everybody goes through this on their wedding day."

"No," Rob said, stopping him. "This is something more. I feel like I am making the biggest mistake of my life. I've got to get out of here, Joe. I can't do it. I just can't."

Rob walked to the door that led to the sanctuary and looked out where more than a hundred people awaited the ceremony. He shut the door and walked to the doors that led to the church exit. He was heading out when Joe stopped him.

"Come on, Rob. Come back in here and sit down. You're going to be fine, and the minute you see Lisa walking down that aisle, you'll be okay."

Rob sat down. Joe brought him a Coke and tried to make him laugh again, talking about things the two of them had done during their years as friends. Rob saw Joe's mouth moving, but he didn't hear the words. He felt like he was going to have a heart attack if he didn't get out of this room and out of his tux. The only thing he could think of was that he wanted to run as fast and as far away as he could get from that church.

Rob's dad and the rest of the groomsmen showed up, and Rob finally began to half-heartedly banter with the guys. When the time came, he took his place at the altar, still hoping he would feel differently once he saw Lisa.

On June 12, 1982, at half past six o'clock, Lisa Outlaw, looking every bit the beautiful bride, walked down the aisle at Middlebrook Pike Methodist Church and became Mrs. John Robert Whedbee. Rob knew he would never quite get over the feeling that he should have run.

CHAPTER 9

Before the wedding, Rob and Lisa needed to find a home where they would start their married life. They found several places they both liked, but the rent was astronomical. It was 1982, and the world's fair was in high gear, attracting visitors from all over the globe. Many landlords had inflated rental prices, hoping to make a fortune from tourists needing accommodations during the fair.

During their apartment search, Rob discovered a little rancher with potential in the Inskip community of Knoxville. It was an older place that showed the wear from years of renters' damage, and the owner was ready to sell. Rob purchased the house for $34,000, leaving them with a very affordable mortgage of $374 per month.

Evenings and weekends, Rob was busy fixing up the place, making repairs and renovations; and when the Whedbees returned from honeymooning in Destin, Florida, they settled into their little home on Winterset Drive.

Despite Rob's earlier misgivings, times were good for the Whedbees. Rob and Lisa were doing well as they adjusted to life on their own. Rob had grown to love Lisa and had hope for their future. Rob was working full time at the agency, and Lisa came on board as a customer service rep for Rob. Evenings and weekends belonged to the carefree couple, and they made the most of their freedom by traveling when they could or just enjoying simple activities such as working in the yard together and grilling out with friends. Their two families got along well and frequently got together for various celebrations. Rob and Lisa were happy, and the future seemed to hold great promise.

Three years into the marriage, Lisa brought up the subject of starting a family. Her mother was driving her crazy, asking when they were going to have children. Now seemed like a good time to think about taking that next step in married life.

With children on the horizon, Lisa was concerned about bringing up children where they currently lived; and in no time, the couple was busy house hunting again. Rob found a nice home at a reasonable price in the Camelot neighborhood of Karns in west Knox County.

Not long after moving in to their new home on Belfast Lane, Lisa announced to the families that she was expecting. The parents were overjoyed, anticipating the birth of their first grandchild. Rob and Lisa were excited about the impending birth.

On April 13, 1986, Justin Robert Whedbee arrived, to the delight of all. He was the perfect blond-haired, blue-eyed boy and a happy, healthy little baby. The grandparents could not get enough of Justin and were always eager to keep him so Lisa and Rob could enjoy some time alone. As the only grandchild, Justin was the star of the center ring.

As most parents will attest, babies quickly turn into toddlers and then little boys. Justin was growing fast, and Rob looked forward to raising his son the way that he had been raised—in a loving family where Justin would learn the strong values that had been instilled in Rob during his own childhood. He spent as much time as possible with Justin, teaching him to fish almost as soon as he could walk and how to swim before the age of three. Early on, Justin showed a real knack for drawing and coloring and spent hours contently creating pictures. He was well-behaved, and Lisa and Rob never hesitated to take him with them when they went to eat at nice restaurants. He also was a good traveler and seemed perfectly happy to entertain himself on trips the family made to Gatlinburg and Florida. Rob loved being with his son and frequently took him to softball games and to the office. Justin showed a great interest in animals and enjoyed trips to the zoo and the Gulfarium in Destin, Florida.

When Justin was born, Lisa quit work with Rob's blessings. They both believed having mom at home was the best way to raise

32

happy, healthy kids. Rob felt Lisa was a good parent and attentive to Justin, but at times, he noticed she could be short-tempered. Rob figured it could be stress from being at home, taking care of Justin all day. She didn't like getting up in the night when Justin was sick or hungry and insisted it was Rob's job since he was gone all day. Rob really didn't mind because he liked spending time with his son for any reason.

For the most part as the last days of the '80s flashed by, the Whedbees—Justin, Lisa, and Rob—had a nice little family. Life was good.

CHAPTER 10

Summer was beginning to slip away in September of 1989 when Lisa brought Rob the news that she was expecting again. They were both thrilled that a second child was on the way, and Justin would have a baby brother or sister to grow up with. It was a time of contentment for both the Whedbee and Outlaw families.

Halloween and then Christmas rolled by, and everything seemed to be going smoothly with the pregnancy. Their doctor had asked if Lisa wanted to have an amniocentesis to determine if the baby had birth defects, but it didn't seem to be necessary, especially since there was a small risk of miscarriage associated with the procedure.

On an icy morning, March 7, 1990, Brittany Alice Whedbee greeted the world. A little girl was a welcome addition, and the families cheered when Miss Britt was born. Rob and Lisa took turns holding their new daughter, and the grandparents were all lined up for their chance to meet the babe.

Later that day, after things had settled down a bit, Rob was sitting in the room with Lisa and Brittany when a nurse entered the room. She went over to the crib and seemed to be taking a long, curious look at the infant.

Somewhat alarmed, Rob asked, "What are you looking at?"

"Oh, nothing, Mr. Whedbee," she answered. "Just looking."

But it wasn't "just nothing" as Rob found out later that day when the doctor came to tell them their beautiful little girl most likely had Down syndrome, and they would need to perform some genetic testing to confirm what they suspected. Lisa was hysterical. She turned to Rob and said, "How do we get out of this?"

Lisa's father, Bill, was standing in the room, and he and Rob were both taken aback. They did their best to calm her, but her hysteria quickly escalated into frantic sobs. Through her tears, she looked intently at Rob and repeated her previous words, "How do we get out of this?"

Rob sat in silence for a moment, the gravity of his wife's words sinking in. *She was serious!* Rob was appalled. He finally looked at her and responded, "Lisa, I don't think this is something we can or should get out of."

Rob's statement only succeeded in fueling her frenzy, and the room filled with a litany of profanity and curses targeted at Rob with the skill of a sniper. Rob quickly decided to move out of the line of fire and excused himself from Lisa's room.

Lisa's father nodded at Rob and said, "Go on. I'll try to talk to her."

Lisa's doctor was right outside the room when Rob stepped into the corridor. Obviously having heard Lisa's outbursts, he asked, "Is everything okay?"

Rob didn't know what to say and stood there, just shaking his head.

The doctor continued, "I know it's hard to receive news such as your daughter's diagnosis. It is news I hate to deliver to new parents. I'm so sorry about your daughter, but she is still capable of doing many things, most importantly giving and receiving love. There's no reason she can't have a good life."

Bill Outlaw joined them in the hallway about that time. Looking at Rob and the doctor, he said, "I think it's just going to take a little while for her to adjust. Right now, she's mad as hell at you and me, and the rest of the world."

The doctor told them that Lisa's reaction, while frenetic, was not totally unexpected. He then went on and said, "Well, I would like to run some additional tests on Brittany. I'm also a bit concerned about your wife's state of mind, and if you agree, I think maybe we should keep her and the baby in the hospital a few more days."

Rob and Bill both nodded in agreement.

"I've got another patient I need to check on, but if you need me, have someone page me from the nurses' station."

The two men thanked the doctor and shook his hand as he left.

Rob and Bill Outlaw got along famously. Rob knew Bill was honest and fair, and as they slowly meandered down the hall toward the waiting room, Rob turned to his father-in-law and reflected out loud, "I never really thought about having a child with handicaps. I always thought that's something that happens to the other guy."

With the "matter-of-fact" demeanor that was Bill's trademark, he turned to Rob and responded, "I guess sometimes it's your turn to be the other guy."

On that day, the news of Brittany's disorder brought some unexpected reactions from Lisa's and Rob's parents. While the four grandparents were getting something to eat in the hospital cafeteria, Lisa's mother, Josephine, frantically approached Rob's father, Lloyd, and asked, "What on earth are we going to tell people?"

Rob's mom, Joyce, was standing beside her husband and witnessed the angry expression that crossed his face. Anyone who knew Lloyd Whedbee knew he never angered easily and would never say a bad word about anyone.

After staring at Jo for a few seconds, Lloyd retorted, "I don't know what you're going to tell people, Jo, but I'm going to say that's my granddaughter. Isn't she beautiful?"

He then turned and walked away without another word. At that moment, Lloyd Whedbee lost all his respect for Mrs. Outlaw.

While Lisa had remained at the hospital, she continued to reject Brittany, refusing to hold her or even look at her. No cajoling from the nurses could break through the wall Lisa was building. Rob spent as much time as he could with Lisa even though he had a demanding job and, more importantly, a son just shy of four years old who also needed him. The grandparents pitched in wherever they could to help, and Rob was grateful. When he visited the hospital, he would always ask to see Brittany and loved to hold that warm little bundle in his arms.

The next day, Bill Outlaw's prophetic words came true when Rob got to be "the other guy" once again. When Lisa's doctor came calling, Rob knew immediately it was with more bad news.

"I'm so sorry," he began, "but we believe Brittany has a heart condition known as VSD or ventricular septal defect."

Rob's heart sank as his concern rose.

"What is that?" he asked.

The doctor went on to explain that VSD is a common congenital birth defect in babies with Down syndrome where one or more holes exist in the wall that separates the right and left ventricles in the heart.

"Without surgery, the hole could expand allowing the heart to pump blood into the lungs and eventually cause cardiac failure. There is a chance that the hole will close on its own as the heart grows, so we'd like to postpone surgery as long as possible…maybe a couple of years."

As Rob tried to comprehend what he had just been told, Lisa sat in bed, looking cold and disconnected from the reality of the situation. Rob, facing his own fears, thought, *How could this get any worse?* But in time, it would.

Despite support from both families and friends, Lisa was not to be consoled. In her mind, this innocent child had destroyed her perfect world. She was understandably scared and didn't think she could rise to the challenge of caring for a child with such special needs. Lisa would struggle with being able to truly accept Brittany for the next four years, and as Brittany's medical problems exacerbated, Lisa withdrew further and further, not only from her daughter but also from her son. Justin became collateral damage.

Rob would always remember the day he brought Lisa and Brittany home. Rob's mom had put together a little homecoming celebration, and Justin had put his heart into making a banner that read, "Welcome Home, Mommy and Brittany!" He was proud of his loving endeavor, but Lisa took one look at the banner, jumped out of the car, stormed up to the porch, tore it down, and threw it to the ground. Justin, not understanding, was destroyed by her action. Lisa sequestered herself in the master bedroom, wanting no part of any celebration related to *that* child.

The next few days were uncomfortable as they waited for the results of the genetic test to determine if, in fact, Brittany was suffering from Down syndrome. Rob felt a sick anxiety, and Lisa was half out of her mind. She stayed in the bedroom, crying most of the time, while Rob was left to care for Justin and Britt, trying to keep life as normal as possible for his little boy and new baby girl.

For a week, a terrible uncertainty hung over them, and then the call came. Tests had confirmed Brittany *was* a Down syndrome baby, and Rob had the task of breaking the news to Lisa, knowing she would not take it well.

She knew, when he came into the bedroom, what he was going to say.

"Is it true?" she asked, and she only had to look at his face to know it was. She jumped from the bed and ran out of the house, screaming at the top of her lungs. Rob was sure she was having a nervous breakdown, and there was no telling what the neighbors were thinking. Poor Justin was terrified. It was impossible for a four-year-old to comprehend what was happening, and Rob worried about Justin and Lisa. Meanwhile, Lisa was only thinking about herself and how she did not deserve this.

Lisa told Rob, "Well, there goes our perfect family."

Rob's blood ran cold. Rob had tried to be compassionate and understanding toward Lisa even though he was also dealing with the impact of caring for a child with severe health issues and needs. Rob was scared and a bit sad about Brittany's diagnosis, but he was still very proud of his little girl and liked to take her out and about.

Joe Anderson, one of Rob's best friends, remembered Rob telling people Britt was going to be the first Miss America with Down syndrome.

CHAPTER 11

During the months that followed Britt's diagnosis, Rob spent as much time as possible with the kids. He was working hard to help grow the family business, but the kids were his main concern. He also did what he could to encourage Lisa, but she was almost beyond reaching. Brittany's birth was the catalyst for a growing discord between Lisa and Rob. The day Lisa first asked if they could put Brittany in a "facility," Rob lost a great deal of respect for his wife. He was going to take care of their daughter, no matter what. Lisa's treatment and attitude about Brittany impacted her ability to get along with Rob. Things would never be the same in their marriage, and it was going to be a bumpy ride for the next few years.

As the first few months passed after her birth, Britt grew, began to crawl, and seemed to be a happy baby, making cheerful noises when playing with Justin, Rob, and the grandparents. Justin especially loved his little sister and was very attentive to her.

One night in June of 1990, Rob was checking to see if Brittany was sleeping and noticed a slight gurgling sound. She had a tiny little nose, and he thought maybe she was snoring. At their next doctor's appointment, Rob mentioned it, asking if it could be the VSD. A trip to the cardiologist confirmed the hole in Britt's heart had enlarged and open-heart surgery would be required. They had hoped to wait until she was older, but at six months of age, Brittany underwent heart surgery. Because the hole was so large, it was necessary to create a patch to sew over the opening, but Brittany seemed to recover quickly. After that, she had a good run. She began to pull herself up, grabbing onto tables and chairs, and by February of 1991,

Brittany Alice was taking her first steps. Her big brother, Justin, like always, was watching over her.

Like most parents of toddlers, Rob and Lisa began childproofing the house again. Rob had bought a child gate to put up at the top of the basement stairs, which were quite steep. Many times when Rob got home in the afternoons, he would find the child gate blocking off the living room, confining Britt and exposing her to the risk of falling down the basement stairs. Rob was deeply disturbed by this, and it became a major point of contention between Rob and Lisa. Rob was beginning to realize Lisa was more worried about Brittany messing up her living room furniture than the possibility of her falling down those stairs, which did eventually happen. More and more, Rob began to think that she cared more about appearances and material things than she did about people, especially her own small children.

Time did nothing to resolve Lisa's inability to accept Britt. She jumped at the chance to leave the kids in the care of the grandparents. She and her father, Bill, were frequently at odds over her attitude about Brittany and her ever-growing neglect of the family. When Bill Outlaw died during surgery to repair an aneurysm in January of 1991, he and Lisa were not speaking. Lisa took his death hard, as did Rob. Lisa's father and Rob had grown close, and Bill seemed to be one of the few people to whom Lisa listened. Rob felt as if he had lost an ally. He thought of Bill as the "shining star" of the Outlaw clan. He was thoughtful and courteous and always thought about others, while the rest of the family seemed to be self-centered and somewhat obnoxious. Most importantly, Bill truly loved Justin and Brittany.

One day, Rob asked Justin if he'd like to spend the weekend with the Outlaws, and he said no.

"I think I'd rather stay home, Dad," Justin replied. "It's just no fun over there since Pap died."

After Bill's death, Lisa immediately adopted the victim's role, withdrawing even further away from family. Rob tried to make her happy, even indulging her at times. He was determined to keep the family strong and together for the kids. As hard as he worked during the day, he often came home to find Lisa gone with Joyce or Jo babysitting for the kids—usually Jo. He would take over and make sure the kids were fed, bathed, and put to bed. He did not mind his fatherly responsibilities; in fact, he enjoyed them. But the feeling that his wife was neglecting her own—not to mention taking advantage of the grandparents—truly troubled him.

Still, there were some good times scattered along the way, times when Lisa seemed to be back to her old self and even more accepting of Brittany. Just after Christmas, Lisa, Justin, and Rob decided to spend a long weekend at the condo they owned in Gatlinburg. Jo Outlaw was caring for Britt while they were away. Lisa and Justin were already settled when Rob drove in after work. He was looking forward to spending time with his family and the relaxing weekend ahead.

He and Lisa had frequently enjoyed time at their condo. It was a spacious and airy place, with a beautiful overlook of the Smoky Mountains. Before Britt was born, they would sometimes leave Justin with one set of grandparents and head up there for some time alone. They often ate at their favorite restaurant, The Peddler, located on the Little Pigeon River in Gatlinburg. On occasion, they would ride the Ober Gatlinburg Aerial Tramway up to the pinnacle of Mount Harrison where the views were postcard perfect.

This Saturday morning heralded a bright, crisp day in the making. Rob had slept well and wanted to get out to enjoy the day and the beauty of the landscape all around them.

"Hey, Justin, how about a hike? You up for it?"

"Yeah, Daddy, I wanna go!"

He picked up his five-year-old, towheaded little boy and swung him around.

Lisa watched in disapproval and said, "Not in the kitchen!"

Rob ignored her comment and asked, "How about it, Mommy? You want to go for a little hike?"

He knew her answer before the "no" came out of her mouth. That was just fine with him; Justin and Dad would have a grand time, and off they went into the woods—father and son doing "guy" things.

Rob and Justin followed a path down through the forest. Justin, ever inquisitive, wanted to know the names of all the trees. He picked up rocks, acorns, and bark as they made their way along. Rob showed him some deer tracks. As always, the two had a good time together on their adventure.

It was several hours before they got back to the condo. Lisa's car was gone, but she had left a note saying she had to go home because Brittany was sick. That was all it said, "Brittany is sick." It was before the days when almost everyone carried a cell phone, but Rob was finally able to reach Lisa at her mother's house.

"What's going on, Lisa?" Rob asked with some alarm.

Brittany had already been through so much.

Obviously upset, she told Rob, "She doesn't seem to be in any pain, but she won't move her left arm. It just hangs there. She's got an appointment with the pediatrician Monday morning, but do you think I should call someone or take her to the ER?"

Rob thought about it before responding.

"As long as she doesn't seem to be in any pain and doesn't have any other symptoms, I think we can wait until Monday. Justin and I will get some lunch and then come on home."

Lisa was relieved, knowing Rob would be there to help make the difficult decisions ahead and help her through this latest nightmare.

When Monday morning finally rolled around, the pediatrician examined Brittany but was at a loss as to what might have caused her condition. He speculated that perhaps she had a stroke, but he thought this was most likely not the case. He advised Rob and Lisa that the problem would most likely resolve itself, which both found to be an unsatisfactory answer.

Over the next several days, Brittany began to exhibit other problems with her coordination. She could not grasp her cup or her favorite toys and seemed to have lost interest in playing. After making some inquiries, Brittany was examined at the East Tennessee Children's Hospital in Knoxville. Numerous tests were run, but all came back inconclusive.

Finally, one neurologist, Dr. Christopher Miller, talked to the parents, explaining that Brittany might be suffering from a rare malformation of the blood vessels in her brain known as Moyamoya disease.

Moyamoya is an extremely rare disorder, not often found in Caucasians and only slightly more prevalent in Asians, although the name is Japanese for "puff of smoke" based on the appearance of the brain in CAT scans of individuals suffering from the disease. A normal person's x-rays will show distinct rivers of blood vessels running through the brain. In a patient with Moyamoya, the vessels are tiny and so close together; they are indistinguishable from each other in an x-ray but appear to look like a cloud or "puff of smoke."

In January of 1992, Brittany was once again facing a serious medical problem. They learned that an arteriogram was the only way to determine if it was Moyamoya disease, and Brittany would have to be put under anesthesia for the test. This concerned Rob since it had only been six months since Britt's heart surgery. He and Lisa decided to hold off on the arteriogram and closely monitor her, watching for any changes in her ability to function.

A week later, Lisa had gone to church, and Rob was home, playing with Justin and Brittany. Brittany had been walking well up to that point. Rob was watching as she maneuvered around the coffee table when she suddenly fell. Thinking she was just playing, Rob picked her up, and down she fell. That was enough to start Rob worrying, and he called the physician's after-hours number. When the doctor returned his call later that day, it was decided to admit Brittany to University of Tennessee Medical Center for the arteriogram on Monday morning. During the procedure, Brittany developed a severe blood clot in her leg that could have killed her and had to be dissolved quickly before the doctors could complete the arteriogram.

Brittany's tests confirmed she did have Moyamoya. The blood vessels in her brain were too small to supply enough blood to it, and they feared brain damage. The doctors did not give the Whedbees much hope for Brittany, basically telling them to take her home and love her because she probably would not be around much longer.

Refusing to give up, Rob and Lisa continued to look for other options. They learned that the Mayo Clinic in Rochester, Minnesota, offered an experimental treatment called an arterial bypass. The Whedbees were advised to submit a letter of diagnosis and Britt's medical records that would be reviewed to determine if she was a candidate for the procedure.

The days trudged by, and the anxiety of the wait did nothing to ease the strain on Rob and Lisa's marriage. Lisa's attitude about Brittany was immensely upsetting to Rob. She often said, "There are places for children like Brittany who require around-the-clock care. She would be taken care of, and we could visit her anytime." Rob remained adamant; if he was physically and financially able to care for Brittany, he would. It was nonnegotiable, and Lisa could accept it, or she could leave.

But if they could only fix Britt, Lisa thought, *I and Rob could once again have the perfect family, which was so important to me. Everything would be good again, if they could only fix her.*

It was a trying time for all involved, and it only fortified Lisa's desire to be free of Brittany. Every time she said something about not being able to take Brittany for another minute, it took Rob back to that first day when the first words out of her mouth were, "How do we get out of this?" What most scared him was that he knew she was serious.

Finally, the Mayo Clinic called with the decision to take on Brittany's case. Rob and Lisa began preparations for their trip to Rochester. By this time, Britt was in a terrible state. She screamed almost incessantly, and the doctor finally prescribed a liquid form of Valium to help her sleep.

On February 12, 1992, Rob and Lisa, carrying their screaming child, boarded a plane for Minnesota. Rob noticed some of the passengers looked particularly intolerant of this disruption. He gave Brittany some more Valium to quiet her down for the trip. As the other passengers stared, Lisa's anger mounted. Rob explained to the passengers closest to them about Brittany's medical condition. None of them were familiar with Moyamoya, and as Rob talked about what Britt had been through, they immediately became supportive and even asked questions about the disease and its treatment.

Rob and Lisa were ill-prepared for the Minnesota weather. Six-foot snowbanks flanked every street, and the icy wind blowing, sometimes at fifty miles per hour, cut through their inadequate jackets like needles. Fortunately, the Mayo Clinic was directly across the street from their hotel, so they braved the cold on their brief morning trek to the hospital.

After studying Britt's medical records and processing insurance, she was admitted, and the doctors immediately began running a battery of tests necessary to proceed with her surgeries. The test results were not good, revealing that Britt had suffered extensive brain damage. On a scale of one to five, with five being the worst, Brittany was about a four. Having hoped for a miracle from the famous Mayo Clinic, Lisa and Rob took the news hard.

The doctor went on to advise them that the only treatment for Moyamoya was arterial bypass surgery, which, in 1992, was still considered to be experimental. The surgery required cutting a hole in the skull above the ear, using an artery from the scalp, and running it inside the skull to the brain in hopes the brain would accept the new artery and reestablish the brain's blood supply, ideally reversing some of the brain damage. The doctors explained it would be a two-part procedure, doing Britt's right side first and then ten days later operating on the left side of her brain. Rob and Lisa were told that recovery time could take as long as two years. The doctors also told the Whedbees the surgeries might not have any effect or, worst-case scenario, she might not survive. After weighing the options, Rob and Lisa decided Brittany's only hope for a more normal life was if she had the surgery.

The surgeries seemed to go well, but it was quite shocking to see her once the bandages were removed. Poor little Britt's head looked like a baseball, with all the stitches. Lisa decided she could not handle the stress of the situation and felt it necessary to return home. Rob stayed behind with Brittany as she recovered. Additionally, Lisa was so distraught; she felt unable to care for Justin, so she left him with Rob's parents, never even letting them know she was back in Knoxville. Brittany celebrated her second birthday at the Mayo without her mother, but she was in her dad's arms, and she was smiling in the picture that was taken.

CHAPTER 12

After their return from the Mayo Clinic, Rob and Lisa were very discouraged with Brittany's progress. Her recovery was slow, and she remained incapacitated for a long time. They had hoped for more signs of improvement after undergoing such a complex and lengthy surgery.

As had been the case since Brittany's birth, family and friends rallied around to provide support to Rob and Lisa. Lisa's mother, Jo Outlaw; Rob's parents, Joyce and Lloyd; and even little Justin all pitched in to help with Miss Britt. But it seemed Lisa became increasingly absent from family life, still unwilling to accept the child she had given birth to.

Rob never complained that Lisa was rarely home. She had joined the Trinity United Methodist Church choir, and Rob's mom, Joyce, often said that every time the church doors opened, Lisa was there. Lisa also renewed her close friendship with her high school friend, Tammy, who was still single and living in an apartment complex in Knoxville. Most weekends, Lisa could be found flaunting her bikini-clad body at Tammy's pool while Rob remained at home, caring for his kids. An investigator from the attorney general's office would later reveal Lisa had a brief affair with a good-looking fellow in law enforcement she had met at the pool. According to rumors from the police department cafeteria, the officer once commented to a fellow officer, "Yeah, I know her. I used to see her, but then I found out she was married, and I dumped her."

Lisa's own mother often asked Rob if he didn't wonder what Lisa was doing. Quite frankly, as the year wore on and Lisa grew more distant from her husband and children, there were times Rob almost hoped she wouldn't come home. Since Brittany's birth, the marriage had not been the same; and during the three years that had traveled by, the fissures and cracks in their union had expanded close to the shatter point.

CHAPTER 13

May 9, 1993, was Mother's Day; and Lisa leaped out of bed, put on her robe, and bounded off as giddy as a little girl on Christmas. She threw open the front door, and there it was—the Sunday edition of the *Oak Ridger*, a small local newspaper. Lisa swept it up and began to tear open the sections, squealing in delight when she saw it, shouting from the cover of the Life and Style section, "A Mother's Nightmare: A Mother's Dream," written by Life and Style editor Michael Frazier. Michael was also the organist and choir director at their church.

Complete with color pictures of Lisa and Brittany, the full-page article told the poignant story of a young mother doing her best to raise a child with Down syndrome. Lisa rushed to the bedroom to proudly show it to Rob.

Rob never claimed to know much about writing, but he did know journalists are supposed to tell the "who, what, when, where, why, and how" and adhere to the facts when they wrote their stories. This article was largely a "puff piece" designed to make Lisa seem like "Mother of the Year." Although Rob and the grandparents were doing the lion's share of caring for Brittany, Rob and Justin were mentioned only briefly in the article. Instead, the story portrayed Lisa almost saintlike as she dealt with the responsibilities of raising a child with special needs on her own. It conveniently skipped over the ugly parts that had transpired since Britt's birth. As had always been the case with Lisa, how things appeared was the important thing, no matter how far from the truth appearances were. There were some honest revelations in the piece as Lisa was quoted verbatim, "It sounds bad, I know, but I was rejecting Brittany. I didn't want to hold her. When people would say, 'She's so cute,' I would think, *She's not cute. She's different."*

The story was well written; Michael Frazier was a gifted writer. It came across more like a fairy tale, but the members of Trinity were enthralled and commended Lisa for the struggle she had faced. The pictures were excellent, showing Lisa loving on Brittany. The little girl looked so cute and happy in a sweet dress her mother had gotten her for the photo shoot. A professional picture of the family was included, and the Whedbees looked like the perfect family.

> "It sounds bad, I know, but I was rejecting Brittany.
> I didn't want to hold her.
> When people would say, '"She's so cute,'"
> I would think, "she's not cute. She's different."
>
> —Lisa Whedbee, *A Mother's Nightmare,*
> *A Mother's Dream,* The Oak Ridger Newspaper

Frazier's account of Lisa's "nightmare" failed to mention some of the prime examples of Lisa's problems with Brittany, neatly sweeping those facts under some magical rug. The article also painted the picture that "poor" Lisa was a heroine, dealing with her "nightmare" on her own, also putting Lisa right where she liked to be—at the center of attention. The story clearly placed Lisa upon a pedestal carved by a mesmerized Michael Frazier. At the time, no one knew Michael's true feelings, which, most likely, had shaped the tone and content of the story.

Rob indulged Lisa her fifteen minutes of fame. On the way to church, Lisa made Rob stop so she could pick up copies of the paper to hand out to friends and family before the service. Fact or fiction, the article would go on to win a prestigious award; but after all was said and done, it would always remind Rob about how distorted newspapers articles could be.

CHAPTER 14

Michael Frazier was not an attractive man—not by any stretch of the imagination. At six feet, he had a scrawny frame and had a slightly humped back, probably from years of leaning over to play the organ. His hair resembled steel wool and was usually in dire need of a good trim. His eyes were beady black holes punctuating his pinched, scruffy face. Unable to wear contact lenses, Frazier's myopia was corrected by large, horn-rimmed glasses that only accentuated a small, taut face with thin, lifeless lips and a receding hairline.

Although plagued by social awkwardness, there were two arenas where Michael had friends and truly excelled—Trinity United Methodist, where he was thought to be a musical genius, and at the *Oak Ridger*, where his talent as a writer was appreciated. Unknown to most, Michael possessed a certain disdain for many people, usually thinking he was the smartest person in a room. He was quick with sarcastic comments veiled as jokes when someone's "stupidity" annoyed him. Like one in three Americans, Michael suffered from bouts of depression, compounded by a certain bitterness stemming from his disappointment in the life he was living.

But Michael Frazier had a secret—one he kept from the world. He was in love with a beautiful creature he had met seven years earlier. His joy, and, paradoxically, sadness, spun around his brain when he allowed himself to fantasize about how his life would be with her by his side. Facing the truth, he knew there was no way such a woman would ever be interested in him. In his heart, he knew Lisa Whedbee was unattainable.

Lisa and Michael's friendship began to grow when she joined the choir in 1991, about a year after Brittany was born. He admired the strength she seemed to show for the cards she had been dealt. He had no way of knowing it was a well-practiced facade she presented to the world. The tender care she showed for her daughter moved him, and he always wished there was some way he could help this precious angel. It was this desire that motivated Michael to suggest the story about Lisa and her struggles to raise a special-needs child.

Lisa loved the idea of the story. Of course, Lisa loved anything that made her the center of attention, and she was happy to meet with Michael numerous times as they worked on the article. Michael was in heaven getting to spend time with Lisa almost every day during the two weeks it took to gather everything he needed to write the piece. Maybe he stretched it out a little bit, but being in her presence made him feel like the man he had always wanted to be. Despite everything he was feeling, he thought he was in tight control of his behavior lest his true feelings slip out and give him away. When the article was published on that Mother's Day, Michael was jubilant to see how proud and happy Lisa was with his work.

Michael would have almost fainted if he knew, for all his outward control, Lisa had become increasingly aware of his feelings for her. She thought his adoration of her was sweet, and she did become fond of him, but, *just maybe,* a thought began to germinate in her mind—perhaps Michael Frazier *could* serve a real purpose in her life.

Wednesday night, late May 1993, choir practice had just wrapped up, and Michael Frazier was doing what he always did at the end of a practice night—putting away hymnals, straightening up chairs, and making notes for the Sunday bulletin.

"Michael…"

The voice was soft and sweet, yet it startled him. He thought he was alone. He turned to find himself lost in Lisa Whedbee's blue eyes.

She reached out, touched his shoulder, and said, "I'm so sorry. I didn't mean to scare you."

"I…I thought…I thought everyone was gone," he stammered.

Regaining his composure as best he could, standing inches from the woman he idolized, he asked, "What can I do for you, Miss Lisa?"

"Can we talk? I need to talk to you." She lowered her head. "I've put this off for so long."

"What is it, Lisa? Is something wrong?"

"Well, it is wrong, but it feels so right," she went on. "For some time now, I've had these growing feelings for you. I know it's wrong, but I can't stop thinking about you."

She raised her head and stared deeply into his eyes.

Michael Frazier was dumbstruck. The hymnal he was holding fell from his hands and echoed upon the wooden floor of the music room. In his mind, he was rewinding the words he had just heard, still unable to believe this moment was real.

"Please say something, Michael," she implored. "I think I love you."

The dam broke, and the words began to flood out of his mouth.

"I can't believe this, Lisa. I think I am dreaming. I've had feelings for you for years and years. My feelings are so strong. It's almost painful to be close to you, thinking I could never have a chance with you. Now you tell me this. Are you really serious?"

"Oh, Michael," she exclaimed gleefully, "I knew there was a chemistry between us. I just knew it. I think we'd be so good together. Do you feel it too?"

Much like awkward teens, they did not touch that night as they walked together to the church parking lot. She was leaving with her family for the beach the next day, but she promised to call him. She blew him a kiss as she climbed into her black Jimmy and drove away. Michael stood there watching long after her lights had disappeared, waiting for the thundering in his heart to subside. This Wednesday night in late May of 1993 was the happiest moment of his life, and he would replay it repeatedly until the day he died.

True to her word, Lisa called Michael three or four times while she was with her family in Destin, Florida. On the phone, they clucked like lovestruck kids. They giggled, gushed, and talked about seeing each other as soon as Lisa returned to Knoxville.

The day Lisa returned from vacation, she and Michael met in a parking lot and talked about how happy they were to be reunited. Several days later, they drove to Chattanooga for the day where they held hands and kissed for the first time. Michael would later say that was the turning point in their relationship. It had become serious. In late July, in Oak Ridge Hotel, Lisa and Michael would attempt to consummate their affair; but much to Michael's embarrassment, he was unable to complete the act. Lisa assured him that their love was what was important, not sex. Unknown to Michael was the fact that Lisa was still sexually active with her husband throughout the duration of their affair.

CHAPTER 15

Summer passed, and by the fall of 1993, Rob and Lisa had grown even farther apart. Rob spent his time earning a living, building his business, and parenting when he wasn't at work. Lisa continued to be more and more absent from family life, now well ensconced in her affair with Michael Frazier.

One night in early October, Rob had finished dinner and put the kids to bed when he began to feel quite queasy. Lisa advised him to lie down, saying he would probably feel better in a little while. But Rob didn't feel better, but much worse. Never one to be sick, Rob felt like something was wrong with him, maybe a stroke or something. He told Lisa how he was feeling, and she suggested he drive himself to the emergency room while she stayed home with the children. Rob, however, was so dizzy, and the pain in his head was thundering. He was in no condition to drive himself anywhere.

"I don't think I can drive, Lisa."

Lisa was underwhelmingly concerned and argued it was too late to bother her parents or Rob's. He could not understand her resistance to taking him to the hospital. Finally, when Rob could no longer stand and was crawling toward the phone, Lisa called her mother. When Jo Outlaw arrived, it took both she and Lisa to get Rob into the car. They spent most of the night at the hospital, and in the morning, Rob was better, but the ER had been unable to diagnose the basis of his problem. Down the line, Rob would remember that night and wonder if Lisa had tried to poison him.

CHAPTER 16

The holidays had come and gone with little incident, and one day in early January, Lisa came to Rob and asked him what he would think about her coming back to work at the agency part-time. If the children were in school or Mother's Day Out, Rob thought it would be fine, and they could always use the help at the busy agency.

Several days later, Lisa said, "You know, since I haven't been active in the insurance business for several years now, I think it would be a good idea to refamiliarize myself with some of the policies and forms."

Rob agreed that made good sense and offered to bring home some books and manuals to review as a refresher, but Lisa said, "I have a better idea. Just bring our personal file home because it has an example of just about every type of insurance."

"That's true," Rob said, and several days later, he brought the files home for Lisa to study.

Lisa dug right into the paperwork, periodically asking Rob questions about certain forms. Rob was pretty sure Lisa knew the answers to her questions but was pleased she was being so thorough as she went back through old territory. Rob fervently hoped this was a good sign for their relationship.

When Lisa had worked at the agency before, she had been licensed to sell and service basic auto and homeowners' insurance, so Rob was somewhat surprised when he saw Lisa had pulled out his life insurance policy. Life insurance requires a separate certification and license.

Rob jokingly asked her, as she was poring over the policy, "Hey," laughing, "are you thinking about bumping me off for my life insurance?"

"Of course not," Lisa answered. "But I know how you're always complaining how difficult it is to sell life insurance. I was thinking about getting licensed to sell life insurance and focus totally on that."

"That would be great," Rob said. "But you know life insurance is a difficult and involved product to explain, much less sell."

"I'd really like to do it," she responded.

And so a couple of weeks flew by, and the file just laid on the dining room table with Rob's life insurance policy on the top of the stack. And finally, Rob asked Lisa if she would like to schedule the life insurance exam.

"Or," he offered, "you could come get some on-the-job training at the office and study for the exam when it's not busy."

Lisa said she would let him know.

Several more weeks passed, and this time when Rob approached her about it, she got very defensive, saying she had decided that she didn't have time to work and take care of the kids.

"I think it's more important that I be available for Justin and Brittany than it is for me to work right now."

Once again, confused by Lisa, Rob shook his head and took the files back to the office, and that was the last time he heard anything about Lisa reentering the workforce.

When February rolled around, Lisa's late nights out were stretching from nine or ten o'clock to eleven or twelve o'clock. Rob often came home to find Lisa's mother, Josephine, taking care of the kids. Jo let Rob know she had been there ever since Lisa picked Justin up from school at 3:30 p.m. When Rob inquired about her whereabouts, Lisa would say, "Oh, I was shopping," or "I was just driving around thinking." She also said on choir practice nights, she, Michael, Tracy, Tammy, and others would go out to a restaurant and hang out. Whatever the story, Lisa began to draw even further and further away from her family.

One afternoon when Rob arrived home from work, Justin met him in the garage and told his dad something in the house smelled bad. Rob found Brittany, barely two and a half years old, in the kitchen sitting in her high chair wearing a diaper that obviously had not been changed all day. The diaper was so soaked that it was dripping on the floor, and poor little Britt was caked in her own waste. Rob was horrified and very upset to know his little girl had been so neglected.

While Rob was changing her, Lisa came into the room looking as if she had just awakened. Rob was angry and told her they needed to talk about the condition in which he had just found Brittany. Lisa protested, saying she had just changed Britt an hour ago. The argument escalated, and Lisa took off in her car and did not return until late that night.

There were other instances that concerned Rob. He had been working in the garage one Saturday while Lisa was standing in the kitchen on the phone with a friend. Justin had stood by her, waiting to ask her if he could go ride his bike in the neighborhood. Growing impatient, Justin finally said, "Mom…." Rob walked through the kitchen door just in time to see Lisa slap Justin across the face with a wet dish towel. Rob was furious. Lisa, oblivious to Rob's anger, continued to talk on the phone until Rob took the receiver away from her and hung it up.

Rob said emphatically, "Don't let this happen *ever* again."

Lisa started to protest, but Rob turned his back to her, took Justin's hand, and took him back outside.

Justin loved his mom, but even at six years old, he could have told his dad other stories about Lisa's treatment of him and Britt. He kept those stories to himself until many years later.

Like many Americans, Rob Whedbee was a strong believer in the Second Amendment—the right to bear arms. He had been a responsible gun owner since his early teens. The guns he collected remained unloaded and safely locked in a gun cabinet in his downstairs den. As an additional precaution, Rob had no ammunition in the house, instead keeping it locked in the trunk of his car.

One February afternoon in '94, Rob was relaxing in his den when he noticed the gun cabinet was empty. His guns were gone. It seemed unlikely they had been stolen, so with displeasure, he asked Lisa about it.

She admitted she had removed the guns from the house but refused to tell him where they were.

"Guns are dangerous," she explained. "I don't like having them in the house, especially having two small children."

Rob was livid and said, "You have no right! Those are my personal property. How would you feel if I took your jewelry and removed it from the house?"

"But guns are dangerous," she countered.

"Guns *can* be dangerous, Lisa, but there is no ammunition in this house. I want the guns back."

Lisa finally agreed to bring the guns back if Rob would agree to put a trigger lock on each of them. She had learned about them in a documentary about a young boy who was killed by a gun kept in his house.

Rob agreed but told her he would need to have the guns in his possession to have them custom fitted by a gunsmith.

When the guns were still missing several weeks later, Rob asked about them again; and a few days later, they were back in the gun case. Rob tried to explain to Lisa the process of fitting trigger locks, but she had no interest and simply told Rob to take care of it.

Two days later, Rob was caught totally off guard when Lisa came to him and said maybe it would be a good idea to have a gun for protection. Rob nearly dropped his teeth. His guns had been a point of contention throughout most of his marriage, and this was the last thing Rob expected to hear from his wife.

Lisa had recently begun watching true crime shows, which were in their infancy at the time. She had seen a show that explored home invasions and explained they were much more common than people thought. Lisa said this had started her thinking maybe Rob was right. She asked which gun would offer the best protection, and Rob had explained a shotgun had the least margin for error. Lisa and Rob then agreed, in lieu of the trigger locks, Rob would ensure there was no ammunition in the house except for a single shotgun shell for the 20-gauge shotgun. The shell would be hidden near the gun case.

Then in a strange twist, Lisa said she needed to know how to use the shotgun in case Rob wasn't home if something happened. Rob was genuinely shocked. For twelve years, he had tried to interest his wife in learning how to use a shotgun, but she had always refused. Could she really be coming around on the issue of home protection?

Rob happily showed her how to load the shotgun chamber with the shell, how to turn off the safety, and how to pull the trigger to fire the gun. Lisa said it seemed easy enough, and it was agreed to hide one shotgun shell on the top of the gun cabinet, well out of sight and reach of any child.

Rob felt good about the outcome of the whole gun incident. Little did he know, it was just the beginning of a cunning plan that would eventually jeopardize his life.

CHAPTER 17

Lisa and Michael had been seeing each other for nine months, and they both were tired of sneaking in and out of motels, meeting in parking lots, and even chancing rendezvous at the Whedbees' home. It was March of 1994 when Michael decided, with great encouragement from Lisa, to rent an apartment for them. So they set up their little "love nest" at Brendon Park Apartments off Cedar Bluff, less than two miles from the home he shared with his wife.

Lisa and Michael frequently discussed divorcing their spouses, but in April of that year, their conversations began to take on a more sinister tenor. Michael would later recount how Lisa began to tell horrid tales of the alleged abuse dealt out by her husband. Michael told how Lisa had described in detail how Rob had pinned her down, forced her legs apart, and raped her. She told Michael she wished she could kill him. Enraged, Michael swallowed hard and mustered all his courage.

"I'll do it. I'll kill him." Something Michael would later attest to saying.

Michael could prove the depth of his love for Lisa and become the hero she so badly needed. He would defeat the monster and save her from the brutality she was supposedly suffering.

Lisa seemed to have no conscience as calculated lies slipped through her lips as easily as a breath.

Michael would later explain how she had said in a terrified voice, "Last night, he got mad at Justin and threw him down on the floor."

Her manipulation was working; he was stepping right into place, just as she intended. He was fitting perfectly into her plans to rid herself of Rob.

Supposedly, when Lisa had tried to intervene, Rob had grabbed her by the neck and thrown her on top of Justin. During all this, Brittany began to cry louder and louder until Rob grabbed her and threw her across the room.

A person with any sense listening to this would have to wonder why such violence had not resulted in injury—severe injury to the two small children. To throw a profoundly disabled little girl across a room would most likely have killed her. Friends and neighbors, who were later interviewed, would adamantly swear there was no way Rob Whedbee could ever do anything like that to the family that he loved so dearly. In the years to come, Justin, then a child of eight, would also confirm that his father had never hurt him in any way, although his mother had no problem slapping him around.

Lisa, however, was on a roll and went on to talk about how she really wanted to kill Rob.

"The last time he raped me, after he fell asleep, I went to the kitchen and got a butcher knife and stood over him while he slept. I was going to do it. I was…but then I just couldn't," she explained. "I'm just not strong enough."

Lisa would continue to tell her tales of rape and abuse, complaining of massive bruises left by Rob's viciousness. She would cry and tremble as she told Michael and later her friends Tammy and Debbie. For all the stories she spun, no one who heard ever thought to take pictures, and no doctor or officer of the law was ever able to substantiate Lisa's claims. In fact, interviews with neighbors, church members, and friends would substantiate that despite the low-cut dresses, bathing suits, and short-sleeve shirts she often wore, no one ever saw a single bruise on Lisa Whedbee.

But Lisa had planted the seed in Michael's head. It seemed, *that's when the conspiracy began*: the fraudulent 911 calls and the trip to the emergency room. An order of protection would later follow. Michael and Lisa were busy laying the groundwork for justifiable homicide. It didn't hurt that Rob was worth more to her dead than alive.

Yes, Michael most likely thought, *Rob Whedbee would have to go*!

CHAPTER 18

In the days of her youth, spent studying at the best schools in Knox County, Lisa learned early on she was different than most of her well-to-do classmates. She didn't have the designer clothes worn by her peers at Bearden, and she was not picked up in a Mercedes or BMW like her classmates. She did not go to cotillion or take ballet lessons. In contrast to the loving household where Rob grew up, there always seemed to be strife and discord in the Outlaw home. Lisa harbored a deep resentment about her lot in life that resulted in a sense of entitlement that she would never shake; it would drive her behavior for the rest of her life.

Somewhere along the way, Lisa Outlaw Whedbee had fallen into total narcissism. That trait was also accompanied by her inability to tell the truth on many occasions to the point of being a pathological liar. She seemed able to say just about anything to get what she wanted, and Lisa wanted a great deal. She had more interest in what she could get others to do for her than what she could do for herself.

Lisa Whedbee was obsessive about her appearance, fretting over her hair for hours and complaining that everything in her very full closet made her look obese. At five feet and six inches and 110 pounds, Rob didn't think there was any way for her to look fat. Rob remembered many times they would be late because Lisa had to look *perfect*.

While appearing to be charming (and she could be) on the outside, Lisa could be quite cunning; and as Rob had long known, she was a good manipulator. Image was everything to Lisa Whedbee, and she invested massive energy in creating the image of the perfect woman, wife, and mother.

Some of Lisa's character defects almost bordered on sociopathy. A sociopath likes to play the victim and will tell stories to make others feel sorry for them, just as she had done when she and Rob were dating and now with Michael Frazier.

At times, Lisa seemed to lack empathy, remorse, and guilt, and nothing was ever *her* fault. She would later tell Justin that the police had framed her. To safeguard their lies, when threatened, a sociopath will suddenly become ill, requiring medical attention. Lisa's phantom illnesses over the years seemed to fit with that.

Maybe Mrs. Whedbee wasn't a sociopath, but she certainly had some form of personality disorder. She was bulldozing her way through life, leaving countless casualties in her wake. They included her husband, both their families, and, most regrettably, her children. She just didn't seem to care, and Michael Frazier was up next.

CHAPTER 19

Martha Walker was sitting at her kitchen table, sipping her coffee and wondering what to do. She felt sick as she considered the problem she was facing. Martha was Joyce Whedbee's little sister, and she'd always been especially fond of Rob who had helped her out during many difficult times in her life. She couldn't get her mind off her nephew, no matter how she busied herself.

Martha was a teacher at A. L. Lotts Elementary School and worked with a talented music teacher named Tracy Doty. Tracy was married to Michael Frazier. Earlier that week, Tracy had confided in Martha that she thought her husband was having an affair. Tracy's first husband had cheated on her, and she knew the signs. Her concerns had been amplified when she discovered a motel receipt in one of Michael's pockets. Although Michael had told her the *Oak Ridger*, where he worked as a journalist, had paid for the room for him to conduct an interview for a story he was working on, his explanation did little to ease Tracy's gut feeling that there was another woman in Michael's life.

Tracy went on to tell Martha that Michael had been seen going into a restaurant with a slender blonde woman. That's when Martha remembered a strange conversation she had had with Rob's wife, Lisa, at one of their recent family gatherings. Martha had been at Rob's parents' house when Lisa had sought her out. Martha had never really liked Lisa, believing she was particularly self-centered. She would put on an act for others, appearing sweet and nice, but Martha knew it was just that: *an act*. Lisa was all about looking good and "me, me, me."

So Lisa sat down and started to chat with Martha.

"Do you ever shop off of Cedar Bluff?" Lisa nonchalantly asked. Martha thought, *What a weird question?*

Lisa went on to explain to her in detail that she had found it much easier to shop in Oak Ridge, excusing her presence in certain areas of town.

"So," Lisa said, "if you ever see me on Cedar Bluff, that's what I'm doing—cutting over to Kingston Pike."

It would later come to light that Michael Frazier had rented an apartment in Cedar Bluff, which served as the couple's "love nest."

For Martha, it all just seemed to add up. Tracy's husband was rumored to be having an affair with a woman who resembled Lisa, and then there was this strange conversation. He must be having it with Rob's wife. Martha felt that she needed to warn Rob, but what if she was wrong? Martha finished her coffee and rinsed her cup in the sink.

But what if I'm right? she thought.

What if she was right and didn't say anything? Martha finally decided she had to share her suspicions with Rob. She went to the phone and dialed the number.

"Martha," Rob said cheerfully, "what can I do for you today?"

"Rob, I'm really heartsick about something, and I don't know if you want to hear it."

"Well, you can't say something like that and then not tell me. What's going on, Martha?"

And the story tumbled out. When Martha had finished talking, there was a long silence on the phone.

Finally, Rob said, "I'm glad you told me, Martha. It's a lot to think about. I guess I need to talk to Lisa. And, Martha, I'd appreciate it if you'd keep this between you and me. I'd rather my parents not know right now."

Martha agreed and told Rob she was sorry to deliver the news to him, but in good conscience, she felt like she had to even if she turned out to be wrong.

Rob hung up the phone and shook his head, thinking that would certainly explain Lisa's frequent absences and late nights out.

But Michael Frazier? He was one of the most unattractive and effeminate men Rob knew. If the rumor was true, Michael was batting way out of his league.

While Rob was standing there in the kitchen, mulling over what he had just heard, Lisa came in and poured herself a glass of tea.

"Lisa, I just heard an interesting rumor," he said.

"Oh, really?" she asked curiously. "What'd you hear? Something juicy?"

"Well, the scuttlebutt down at A. L. Lotts is that you and Michael Frazier are more than friends."

Lisa never even flinched and replied indignantly, "Oh *please*, give me some credit. If I was going to sleep with someone besides you, it certainly wouldn't be Michael Frazier. You know we're just friends. I don't see how you could think I could ever be attracted to Michael."

Rob was inclined to believe her.

"Who told you that?" she asked.

"Does it matter?"

"Yes, it matters. I need to put an end to that rumor before someone gets hurt."

"Tracy Doty said something to Aunt Martha…"

Before Rob could finish, Lisa had grabbed the phone and was dialing Martha's number.

"Martha, this is Lisa. Rob just told me what you heard, and I just wanted to thank you for alerting us to this nasty rumor. I am just appalled that someone would think I am having an affair with Michael Frazier. He's my handbell teacher, and I am his student. And really…what would I ever see in Michael Frazier?"

After thanking Martha profusely, Lisa hung up the phone.

"I think I should call Tracy. I certainly don't want her thinking I'm sleeping with her husband!"

Rob would later find himself stunned and revolted at Lisa's ability to lie so persuasively and with such ease. For the rest of his life, he would question almost everything she had ever told him. Rob was just one of the people who had fallen victim to her lies and manipulations.

CHAPTER 20

Divorce was an ugly word to Rob Whedbee, but it was a word that had been batted back and forth between him and Lisa on more than one occasion during the first months of 1994. Lisa thought they should consider it. Despite the alleged affair and Lisa's growing distance, Rob wanted to keep the family together for the kids' sake.

It was also hard for Rob to give up on his marriage after twelve years. Having been brought up in a loving home with parents who had made a good life together, Rob hated to face the fact that his marriage was looking more and more like a failure. The thought of admitting it to his parents was even harder.

One morning, when looking at the checkbook for the bank account that he and Lisa shared, Rob was not overly surprised to see an appointment card for one of the leading divorce attorneys in Knoxville. When Rob asked Lisa about it, she was very open saying yes, she had scheduled an appointment to discuss her legal rights and position as a nonworking spouse with two children. After discussing it for a little while, Lisa suggested he go with her so that he too could "learn the ropes," so to speak.

The appointment was for Monday, April 11, and Rob was running late. When he arrived at the offices of Sarah Sheppeard, Lisa was already in with the attorney.

"I'm Rob Whedbee," he told the receptionist. "I'm here to see my wife."

Rob noticed the girl looked a bit uneasy, but she asked him to wait while she got someone he could speak with. She called Ardis Kaufman, Sarah Sheppeard's paralegal.

If Rob had known more about the process of divorce, he would have known the last thing a divorce attorney wanted to see was the spouse of a client showing up during a consultation; so naturally, Ardis was somewhat alarmed when she got the call about Lisa Whedbee's husband standing in the waiting room.

As Ardis walked down the long hallway to the waiting room, she could see Rob. He appeared to be very tense, and Ardis felt a bit intimidated.

"Hello, Mr. Whedbee, what can I do for you?" the paralegal asked.

Rob extended his arm to shake hands with Ardis, all very professional.

"I'm here to see my wife," Rob answered.

"Ms. Sheppeard is in conference with your wife right now, but I'll let her know you are here. Please have a seat while I speak with her."

Rob continued to stand, waiting nonchalantly for the paralegal. He thought nothing of it, and maybe they were finishing discussing some matters before they brought him into the room.

Ardis slipped into the main conference room where Lisa, accompanied by her ever-loyal friend, Tammy, was talking with the attorney. She quietly said, "Lisa's husband is here."

Lisa immediately jumped up and said, "I'll see him."

"No, Lisa, I'll handle this," Ms. Sheppeard said as she rose and headed toward the waiting room.

"Mr. Whedbee, this is highly unethical. You cannot be here."

"I just want to see my wife. She told me about this appointment and said I should go with her."

"I'm sorry, but you can't be here. I must ask you to leave. You can see your wife after our appointment."

"But I'm here to meet my wife," Rob said again. "She asked me to be here," he continued, but the attorney stopped him.

"Mr. Whedbee, I'm not prepared to argue with you about this. If you don't leave, I'm afraid I will be forced to call 911."

Rob was getting confused and frustrated, but he shook his head and said, "All right, I'll leave."

He turned and walked out of the office. Halfway to the parking lot, Rob realized he had left his keys in the attorney's office. When he returned to retrieve them, Sarah Sheppeard was still in the waiting room and was shocked to see him return.

"Mr. Whedbee, am I going to have to call 911?"

The receptionist sat, holding the phone poised to make the call.

"I'm just getting my keys," he said. "This has just been a misunderstanding, and I'm sorry."

Confused and upset, Rob decided to drive home and wait for Lisa. Jo Outlaw was at the house watching Brittany, and they discussed the situation. Jo assured Rob it was probably just a miscommunication.

"Yeah," Rob said. "I think she was trying to sucker punch me and make me look like an idiot."

When Lisa arrived home, she appeared to be confused about the situation as well.

Rob asked, "Why'd you let them run me off without explaining that you invited me to join you?"

"I tried to explain," Lisa protested, "but they wouldn't let me. They just kept saying you couldn't be there."

Rob wasn't buying it and asked, "Why are you lying to me in front of your mother?"

This infuriated Lisa. As had become commonplace, she stormed off to the bedroom with Rob behind her, and there they continued to argue about what had happened.

Suddenly, out of nowhere, Lisa said, "By the way, you never did get those trigger locks like you promised. So when you get home tonight, your guns will be gone."

"What?"

Rob started to explain she was the one who had told him he didn't need to go through with that, but he decided any further conversation was futile.

As he left the room, he turned and said, "I'll save you the trouble. I'll just take them to the office and leave them there so you won't have to worry about them anymore."

Rob headed downstairs and was just unlocking the gun cabinet when Mrs. Outlaw appeared. Somewhat alarmed, she asked Rob what he was doing.

"I'm taking my guns to the office so I don't have to listen to Lisa's crap about taking my guns somewhere and hiding them."

"Rob," Jo Outlaw said, "just go back to work and forget about it. I'll make sure Lisa doesn't take your guns anywhere. You can take them to the office tomorrow when all of this settles down." Mrs. Outlaw went on to say, "I don't know what's going on with you two, but you need to decide what to do before this gets out of hand. The two of you need to think about those babies before you decide."

He and Jo might have had their issues, but Rob could not have agreed more with her. He nodded and went to his car and headed back to the office. On the drive back, he thought he should have handled things differently. If he had it to do over again, he would have called the attorney himself beforehand. As far as the guns, he had to admit he really didn't want to show up at the office with a trunk loaded with guns and have to explain. He also didn't want to take them to his parents and burden them with all this craziness, and quite frankly, Rob hated to admit to his folks what a mess his marriage had become.

Rob thought about the stress he'd been under since Brittany's medical issues had exacerbated. He was doing his best to work and build the business and take care of two kids, one with special needs. Lisa was really beginning to wear him out. He felt like the intense stress negatively affected his judgment to the point where he was losing his ability to reason. Some days, he was just happy to survive. Maybe it was time for him to seriously consider separating from Lisa. Maybe his and the kids' lives would be better without the constant craziness that accompanied Lisa. One thing was for sure—Rob was not happy, and as they say, "Life is too short."

CHAPTER 21

It was a Saturday in early May and a slow day at Knox County E-911 Dispatch. The radio sputtered sporadically with officers checking in, but the phones were unusually quiet. Dispatchers Beth Jarvis and Sandy Carroll were chatting about their plans for that night when line one broke the silence. Beth pushed the record button as she answered the phone.

"E-911. What's your emergency?"

A man's breathless voice exclaimed, "My neighbor's beating the hell out of his wife again. I think he's gonna kill her this time." The excited caller continued, "He's crazy. He tried to shoot a dog last week. Better hurry."

"Sir, what's your location?" Beth queried.

"Their address is 7600 Belfast. It's the house on the right corner."

Before Beth could get any additional information, the line went dead.

"Charlie 14, we've got a possible 10-94 at 7600 Belfast. Can you respond?"

"Ten-four, dispatch. I'm enroute to the address. I'll also need a female officer to assist."

Officer Margie Mahaffey[2] radioed in that she would rendezvous with Officer Segers[3] at the location. She gunned the engine as she turned on to West Emory.

---

[2] The name has been changed to protect the anonymity of the individual.
[3] The name has been changed to protect the anonymity of the individual.

Spring had begun, and the azaleas boasted full blooms of coral, pink, and purple. The dogwoods were decked in holy white, and warm temperatures made it a delight to be outside on an afternoon in Knoxville. Rob was out enjoying the weather, sweeping the front porch on that Saturday.

Rob was curious when he saw two Knox County Sheriff's cruisers coming down the street at a pretty good clip. He was quite surprised when the cars both pulled in his driveway. Getting out of the vehicle, one of the deputies asked Rob if this was 7600 Belfast; and as he was joined by the other officer, they seemed to be approaching Rob warily with their hands hovering above their guns.

Rob informed them that his address was 7500 Belfast Lane and was wondering just what was going on at 7600 Belfast. It must be something big! Rob expected them to leave to go find 7600, but they insisted they had the right house. Rob was confused and a little bit irritated when they asked if anyone else was home and if they could search the house. Rob told them they were welcome to look around, but he was the only one home.

"What makes you think you have the right house?" Rob asked one of the officers.

"Isn't this the first house on the right corner?" Officer Segers asked.

Rob answered yes, which seemed obvious. Rob started to follow him in and asked them if they would like some tea. Segers replied no and asked Rob to wait outside with his partner, Officer Mahaffey. Rob said okay but still thought that it was awfully weird, especially since they obviously had the wrong house.

He thought to himself, *They're really wasting time when they should be taking care of business at 7600.*

Rob made small talk with the female officer as they waited on the porch. Rob continued to sweep, looking for the other deputy to return. About five minutes later, the other officer came out of the house and looked at Officer Segers, shaking his head.

"There's no one inside." He turned to Rob and said, "Sorry to have bothered you, sir."

They walked to their cruisers and one drove off. As Officer Segers was about to get in his cruiser, he looked over the top of his car and said to Rob, "I really don't know what is going on here, but if I were you, I'd be careful."

Rob nodded and still didn't think much about it, staunchly convinced they had the wrong house. He was still wondering what the heck was happening over at 7600 that was causing trouble when Lisa rolled up. Rob told her about what had happened, and she innocently agreed they must have had the wrong house.

Knox County Sheriff's detectives would later discover the anonymous call was one of three made that week. It was made by Michael Frazier from a pay phone at Weigel's on Oak Ridge Highway. Rob would later learn that three fraudulent phone calls had been made and surmise that Lisa and Michael were making an attempt to get a record of 911 calls related to the Whedbee house, but Frazier had screwed up on his timing, calling before Lisa had even gotten home. Still, it had to be just another piece in the premeditation and conspiracy puzzle they were building.

As they left, Rob noticed they went to his next-door neighbor's house, the Shinn's, and knocked on the door, but no one was at home.

CHAPTER 22

Sunday, May 15, started as a gray day. It was a routine Sunday in the Whedbee household. Rob was busy getting Justin and Brittany ready for Sunday school at Trinity United Methodist Church. As usual, Lisa was fussing over her hair, her makeup, and what to wear. Because Lisa sang in the choir during the church service after Sunday school, it was customary for both Rob and Lisa to drive their own cars. Rob would frequently take Justin fishing or to ride bikes after Sunday school, and Brittany would typically stay in the nursery during the church service. Lisa would bring Britt home, and the family would have Sunday dinner between one thirty and two o'clock.

That day, the routine was somewhat different. Justin was going to swim at Rob's parents' pool, so Rob stayed for church. At the last minute, Rob's dad, Lloyd, asked if Brittany could also come along. Rob was going to check with Lisa, but the choir door was already closed, so he saw no problem in letting Britt accompany her brother for some fun in the grandparents' pool and give the couple the much-needed alone time. Rob said goodbye to Justin and Brittany and went back in to sit down for church.

After church, Rob was standing in the hallway talking with some friends when Lisa, still wearing her choir robe, came down the hall looking rather angry.

"Where is Brittany?" she demanded to know.

Before Rob could finish explaining, Lisa stormed off obviously upset. When she came back down the hallway, she barreled past Rob and went straight to her car. Rob followed her and suggested they go out to lunch since they were kid-free for the afternoon.

"I'm not going anywhere with you," Lisa shouted.

Rob was dumbfounded and asked, "Are you mad at me because I let Brittany go with my folks? For God's sake, Lisa, I just let her go swimming at Mom and Dad's."

"You had no right to let her go without checking with me!" she snapped.

"You were in the choir room with the door closed. It's not exactly the crime of the century for crying out loud."

At this point, Lisa slammed the door of her Jimmy and tore out of the parking lot as startled church members looked on.

Rob shook his head as he got in his car to head home. Little did he know, the fireworks were just beginning. When he arrived home, Lisa was putting ribs in a pot on the stove. When she saw Rob, she headed off to the master bedroom and closed the door behind her. Rob decided it was probably best to let her cool off for a while and gave her some space. Eventually, he went to the door and knocked. He could hear her on the phone and heard her say, "I've got to go. Rob is at the door." She opened the door, and seething, she asked, "What do you want?"

"I'd like to get out of these dress clothes. Do you want me to cook the ribs now?"

Lisa was holding to her anger like a leech on blood.

She said, "I don't care what you do. I'm going downstairs to do some laundry."

Rob watched her storm off, still totally confused as to why she was so irate over such a simple thing. Brittany frequently went to his parents' house for a swim. It was just another confusing and upsetting occurrence of events—something that had become a regularity at the Whedbee household.

Noticing a few pieces of dirty clothing Lisa had missed, Rob decided to take them downstairs to the laundry room. Lisa was nowhere to be found, nor was the laundry running, so he laid the clothing on the washing machine and turned to go back upstairs. Passing by the entrance to the den, Rob got the shock of his life. Lisa was standing in the middle of the room brandishing one of his shotguns. Knowing there was no ammunition in the house, Rob was not overly concerned at first. He did not believe the gun was loaded, so he turned on the light and approached her.

As she raised the shotgun and pointed it at his chest, she said, "Buddy, you've gone too far this time. I'm through with you!"

"You mean you're going to shoot me because I let Brittany go swimming?"

Rob's head was telling him that the gun could not be loaded, but there was something in her eyes that scared him. His feet were telling him to get the hell out of the house, and Rob took off, thinking the whole time, *I'm being chased out of my own home by a crazy woman with my shotgun because I let my daughter go swimming.*

No keys and no money, Rob found himself at a pay phone at Hardee's, maybe a half mile from the house. Thoroughly humiliated, he had to ask a man in the parking lot for a quarter. Standing by the pay phone staring at that quarter, Rob realized his dilemma. He could call his parents and tell them the truth about what was going on in his marriage, or he could try once more to reason with the woman who was his wife. In retrospect, Rob would know he made the wrong decision, but his pride made it hard for him to admit to his folks the lie he was living, and so he called Lisa.

When she answered, he spouted, "What the hell is going on with you and the shotgun?"

She countered, "I don't know what you mean, and you can't prove it anyway. Where are you?"

Rob told her he was at the Hardee's down from the house, and she asked if he wanted to walk back or if she should come get him.

"Are you finished threatening me with my shotgun?" he asked.

Again, she told him she did not know what he meant. Rob finally gave up and asked her to pick him up. Once home, Rob immediately went to the gun cabinet, and there was the shotgun sitting in its usual place, like nothing had happened. Rob wished it had been a bad dream. Just to satisfy his curiosity, he took the gun from the case to reassure himself it had not been loaded.

Lisa came into the room and asked sarcastically, "What are you going to do? Shoot me?"

"No," Rob answered. "That's your game, not mine."

Just as soon as the words had left his mouth, he opened the chamber, and a live 20-gauge shell popped out. He looked at the safety; it was off—. All Lisa would have needed to do to blow his head off, was to pull the trigger.

When the shotgun shell hit the floor, Lisa immediately dove for it like a grizzly bear fishing salmon. Rob instinctively thought if she wanted it so badly, there must be some reason, so he grabbed her by the wrist to make her release the shell. At this point, Lisa started kicking and beating on Rob with her free arm and screaming hysterically. When Rob finally freed the shell from her grasp, he realized it was a Winchester brand shell, and he had always only stocked Federal.

Where did the shell come from?

At that point, Lisa went ballistic, slamming the cabinet door shut and unleashing a tirade of profanity. She was completely out of control, turning over furniture and waving a fire poker at Rob and then at the TV as if she was going to smash the screen. Midswing she stopped. Possessed by another thought, she put down the poker. Lisa marched over to the bar and picked up the cordless phone. With venom in her voice, she announced, "I'm going to call Mom, and you can explain how you just broke my arm, you bastard."

Rob had no intention of talking with Jo Outlaw after the struggle he had just been through, so when Lisa dialed and then tossed him the phone, he pushed the hang up button.

"I don't think you need to involve your mother in this, *and* I didn't break your arm," he said as he handed the phone back to her.

Lisa again dialed a number and tossed the phone back to Rob again. This went on several more times until Rob finally hung up the phone for the last time, placed it in the dock, and turned to go back upstairs. He'd had enough game playing and stress for one afternoon. He told Lisa she needed to either compose herself or go to her mother's. The kids would be home soon, and they didn't need to be around this kind of behavior.

Enraged, she followed Rob halfway up the stairs, screaming and yelling obscenities. Rob immediately took the shotgun shell and placed it under the spare tire in the trunk of his Lincoln, still wondering where Lisa had gotten the Winchester shell. *Had she really*

*planned to kill him? And why was it so important that Brittany be home?
Was her life also in danger?*

Frazzled and worried about the events of the afternoon, Rob
sat on the couch in the den and tried to calm down. Lisa, however,
was not going to let it go and came upstairs still screaming about
her "broken" arm. About the same time, there was a knock at the
door, and Rob got up to answer it, thinking it was his parents with
the kids. He was in for another surprise on that awful day. Instead
of Brittany and Justin, Rob opened the door to two Knox County
officers, one man and one woman.

"Are you the resident of these premises?" the female officer
asked.

Rob nodded as he let the officers into the foyer. Lisa was standing behind him at this point.

"Did you call 911?" the male officer asked, and Lisa jumped out
and said yes.

"What seems to be the problem?" the officer continued.

"My wife and I have been having an argument," Rob replied.

At that point, the female officer led Lisa back to the bedroom,
and the male officer took Rob in the living room where he examined
Rob's neck and hands and then asked Rob to remove his shirt so he
could check for marks. There were none.

The female officer returned to the living room with Lisa and
reported to her partner that she had not found any marks or injuries.

"What's going on here?" one of the officers asked, taking out a
small pad and pen.

Rob proceeded to tell them about the shotgun incident and
offered to show them the shell that had been loaded in the gun, but
they declined, saying since both he and Lisa had access to the gun,
the shell would have little meaning. He did ask if the gun was still
loaded.

"I think one of you should go somewhere for the night...to a
relative's or a friend's," the female officer suggested.

With the kids expected home any minute, neither Rob nor Lisa
wanted to leave. The officers then recommended one of them stay

upstairs and the other downstairs and have as little contact as possible for the rest of that day.

"If we have to come back here tonight," the male officer said as they were leaving, "one of you will be going to jail."

CHAPTER 23

Rob was relieved when Monday morning arrived, and he could escape the high tension at home for the routine of the office. His respite didn't last for long when later that morning Lisa called and asked Rob to meet her for lunch.

Rob was shocked and told her, "I really don't believe what I'm hearing. Last night, you tried to shoot me. Then you called the cops on me. And now you want to have lunch with me? Are you trying to drive me nuts?"

"No," she answered, "I've got something I need to show you."

"Lisa, I'm slammed over here. Can't this wait until tonight?" Rob said in exasperation.

"No," she answered.

It was the typical Lisa, demanding to have her way, and though it was the last thing Rob wanted to do, he once again gave into her, swearing to himself it was the last time.

Rob arrived at Ruby Tuesday first and sat down at a table to wait for Lisa. About five minutes later, she arrived sporting a black Velcro wrist brace—the kind they give you for carpel tunnel syndrome—on her left arm.

Flashing the brace in front of Rob's face, she explained, almost bragging, that she had gone to the ER at St. Mary's that morning.

"I told them you tried to break my arm."

Rob was livid.

"You've got to be kidding me. You got me out here to show me this crap? And if I broke your arm, where's the cast, and how come the brace is on the *wrong* arm? Yesterday, it was your right arm."

"It's not the wrong arm," she said indignantly, "and it's not broken. It's just badly sprained."

Rob had had all he could take. This, on top of the weekend, he had just lived through.

"This is bullshit," he said as he walked off. *More bullshit,* he thought.

Surprisingly, when Rob got home, Lisa was cooking dinner without the arm brace.

"Where's your brace?" he asked.

She replied she did not want to upset Justin by wearing it in front of him. The St. Mary's Hospital report would later reveal that Lisa had told them she fell down the stairs injuring her arm; however, an examination and x-ray showed a perfectly normal left arm.

Lisa was obviously up to something. Rob knew he wasn't being paranoid, but he didn't realize the scope of the travesty that was unfolding.

CHAPTER 24

In Knox County, an Order of Protection is easier to get than grits at a southern diner. In many cases, they're not worth the paper they are printed upon. Anyone can go down to the Division IV Circuit Court, fill out some forms, and write a statement of complaint. Boom—just like that, a legal document is generated without any kind of proof or validation of the claims made by the petitioner.

That's just what Lisa did on Tuesday, May 17, two days after pointing Rob's loaded shotgun at him. Lisa's complaint told a lurid tale of spousal rape and abuse, but she made a few mistakes in her recounting of the abuse she has allegedly suffered.

Her statement read: "On May 15, Rob let me know he felt my body belonged to him. I tried to fight him off…and was bruised on my legs, and my left arm was sprained, bruised, and swollen. Police responded…I got medical treatment for my arm Monday morning."

On May 15, the police did respond to the several hang-up calls from 7500 Belfast, and other than an arguing couple, they found no marks, bruises, or other signs of physical abuse on Lisa or Rob. And, once again, the medical records from St. Mary's, where Lisa sought medical treatment, showed that after x-rays and a thorough exam, the left arm looked perfectly normal. The ER doctor would later say, "If I'd seen signs of abuse, it would have been in my report."

Rob was served with the petition and ordered to appear in court at a hearing. On June 2, at Lisa's request, the order was changed to allow social contact, which meant Rob would continue to live in the residence they both shared. If Lisa was traumatized by Rob's abuse, why would she want Rob anywhere near her or their kids? Lisa knew very well that Rob was not the abuser she had so graphically painted him to be. In fact, Rob was actually the victim of Lisa's verbal and emotional abuse that later, that abuse, would escalate to include violence.

While domestic violence is a very real crime in the United States, with one woman being assaulted every nine seconds, there is a flip side to this coin: 80 percent of domestic abuse allegations against men are false. Both are hard statistics to swallow. Also, one in seven men will suffer some type of abuse during their life.

In court on June 2, before the Honorable Bill Swan, Rob told the judge there had not been any violence on his part.

Judge Swan cut Rob off quickly saying, "Mrs. Whedbee is the one who filed the order, and she's the only one who can agree to it, so I suggest you sit down and be quiet."

Judge Swann thought he'd heard it all, but when Lisa Whedbee asked that the order be changed to include social contact, he could not believe his ears. Social contact would allow Mr. Whedbee to remain in the house they shared on Belfast.

He asked, with raised eyebrows, "Are you sure about that, Mrs. Whedbee?" *If this woman had been so violated by her husband, why would she want him anywhere near her or their kids?*

Lisa affirmed her request, and though Judge Swann, gazing over his half-lens glasses, stared at her in disbelief. Still he allowed it anyway.

Rob signed the document but got the last word in, saying he had never, nor would he ever, abuse his wife. And it was true. Despite Lisa's repeated provocations, Rob had never hit her and had no intention of ever doing so. Lisa had another piece of justification for murder, and she was quite pleased with herself. As for Rob, he was at the breaking point.

After court, Lisa once again shocked Rob by inviting him to lunch; and for some reason, Rob felt compelled to go. As they waited for their sandwiches, Rob asked Lisa why she was making things so hard on him.

"I don't know," she answered. "I'm just so angry. I'm just angry at everyone—you, your parents, just everyone. It seems like nobody cares. You just go on like nothing ever happened, just like Brittany is normal."

Rob responded, "I'm not trying to make you angry, but I don't know any other way to treat Brittany. She is our daughter."

After lunch, Rob was driving down Kingston Pike toward the office.

He thought, *I don't believe I'll ever be able to put this train back on the track.*

Rob conceded that he might as well give up. The marriage was obviously over. If it hadn't been for the children, he would have been gone a long time ago.

That night after work, Rob was thrown another curveball when Lisa came to him to talk.

"Since we had lunch today, I've been doing a lot of thinking. I want things to be like they used to be, before Brittany and all her problems. I don't know what's wrong with me. But I want to try and make things right." She paused and then said, "What do you think about that?"

To say Rob was skeptical would have been an understatement. After all, Lisa had put Rob through a living hell, but Rob wanted to believe it. More than anything, he wanted to provide a stable home-life for Justin and Brittany. That was what he had wanted all along.

Lisa was very convincing, and Rob was hoping against hope she had a change of heart. He agreed to give it a try.

Rob was not yet aware that Lisa was simply putting the finishing touches on her plan. She was lulling Rob to sleep, setting him up for the final chapter of deceit and betrayal. As far as Lisa was concerned, Rob Whedbee, her husband of almost thirteen years, was a dead man.

CHAPTER 25

The sky was dusky violet when Rob arrived home. He pulled his Lincoln in and parked it behind his '84 Corvette. The game had been good. He hadn't played ball with the boys in a long time. He loved the solid crack that echoed off the bat when the ball was hit just right, and it was nice to know he could still knock one out of the park.

The outing had provided Rob with some much-needed stress relief. Things at home had been turbulent and confusing for quite some time, and for the first time in months, he felt a sense of relaxation. He sat there savoring that feeling for a moment before going into the house where he never knew what to expect anymore.

It was eight thirty when Rob came through the garage door into the kitchen. He was famished and quickly spotted a bucket of KFC on the counter. Sitting down at the kitchen table to eat, he wondered what drama Lisa would be doling out that night.

Finishing up his cold chicken, he went down the hall to see his four-year-old, Brittany. Lisa was on the bed reading to her. Rob was surprised to see Brittany already ready for bed. Lisa usually waited for him to come home and change her.

"Hi," Lisa said pleasantly. "You know Justin stayed over with your folks?"

"Yeah. I'm surprised Britt didn't stay with them, too."

"Well, she's been asking for Da-Da all day. Want to play with her for a little while?"

"Sure," Rob answered.

Although he logged many hours at work, he enjoyed spending time with the kids whenever he could.

"Da-Da," Brittany called out happily, reaching for him with the one arm she could still use since her stroke.

Sitting down next to her on the bed, he hugged her.

"Have you been a good girl today, Miss Britt?"

Although Brittany's vocabulary only included a few one-word responses, she nodded her head and said, "Yep!"

"Well, then let's read a story."

Rob picked up *Goodnight Moon* and began to read to her. After he finished the book, they played with some of her stuffed animals. It was nine thirty when he tucked her in, kissed her good night, and closed the door to her darkened room.

"Sweet dreams, Miss Britt."

Down the hall, in the master bedroom, Rob could see Lisa painting her fingernails. He went back through the kitchen and into the dining room to tackle some of the paperwork he'd brought home from the office as he did most nights.

Engrossed in his work, Rob did not hear Lisa enter the room behind him. She was wearing a red silk nightie she had not worn in a long time. It revealed her shapely legs and a good bit of cleavage. There was no denying she was a head-turner.

She began to massage his neck and shoulders and then asked in a flirty little voice, "Are you going to work all night, or are you coming to bed?"

Rob was speechless. He knew the code, but the marriage had been so strained since Britt's birth. It had been a long time since they had been intimate. Her invitation felt like a safe harbor during a storm.

Rob followed his wife to their bedroom. He was thinking about the conversation they had recently. She had told him she had changed her mind about getting a divorce and wanted to try to work things out.

Maybe she really was serious.

Rob stripped down and slid beneath the crisp, cool sheets on his side of the bed. She immediately reached over to him and began to softly run her fingers through his hair, across his chest, and down his thighs.

She kissed him and said, "Now, doesn't that feel better?"

She then straddled him, and the sensations of pleasure washed over Rob.

The sex was good, damn good. They rocked rhythmically together, pushing each other closer to the edge, both climaxing in a crescendo of delight. Once satisfied, they fell away from each other, lying there, each trying to catch their breath.

Rob felt great, turned to his wife, and said, "You know, Lisa, we could make this thing work. If we both try, things could be good again."

She murmured and smiled at her husband. Feeling hopeful, Rob got up to get some water from the kitchen, and Lisa went into the bathroom.

Sitting on the couch in the family room, Rob sipped his water and thought about their marriage. After all the strife between them, the disagreements over Brittany's care, her neglect of both Justin and Brittany, the volatile arguments, the talk of divorce, the order of protection, *could they really make it work?* Maybe he was crazy, but he hoped so.

Rob finished his water and stopped by Britt's room to check on her. When he returned to bed, it appeared Lisa was already asleep. He got under the covers and soon was asleep.

She lay beside him, feigning sleep, anxiously waiting for his breathing to slow. According to Rob, she could have won an Oscar for the performance she had just delivered. Lisa Whedbee wanted out, and the time to execute her plan was at hand.

The horses were at the gate, and Lisa Whedbee was poised for a perfect trifecta.

CHAPTER 26

After she was certain Rob was asleep, Lisa continued to lie there, staring up at the ceiling. Was she thinking about the grand scheme she had masterminded? If all went according to plan, (and no one could possibly know how far her plan extended) she would be a free woman who could afford to do just about anything she desired.

As the clock rolled around to 12:15 a.m., she decided it was time and quietly slipped out of bed. Still wearing her sexy, little nightie, she made her way down the hall and then downstairs to his hiding place.

She opened the door, and he stood up, alert and ready.

"It's time, Michael. I need you," she said in almost a whisper.

"I'm scared," he responded. "Are you sure about this? What about Brittany?"

She wrapped her arms around him and hugged him tightly.

"I'm scared too, but just think of everything we'll have once this is done. I won't have to live in fear. He'll never hurt me again, and you and I can be together forever, with enough money to do or go anywhere we want…and you don't need to worry about Brittany. She won't wake up."

She kissed his neck and whispered, "You and me together forever."

"Okay," he said. "I'm ready."

He already had on latex gloves, and he pulled the black stocking mask over his head. He clutched the knife she had given him earlier and took a long look at it. He was doing this for Lisa, first and foremost, but the money that would come was also motivating. They would have a magnificent life together.

She kissed him and said, "I'll be on the couch upstairs. Make it quick and sure. I'm depending on you."

"Quick and sure," he echoed.

He looked back at her as he ascended the stairs and then stealthily moved toward the bedroom where Rob lay sleeping.

Lisa had partially opened the blinds, and fragments of light from the streetlamp outside poured across the bed, giving Michael enough light to see Rob. His hands were wet inside the gloves from his profuse sweating. His heart was thundering like horses racing on a hard track. He was afraid he might awaken his target. He had to hurry.

He raised the long knife above his head, readying himself to strike. As his arm arced downward, he most surely thought to himself, "*I can do this. This is for Lisa.*"

CHAPTER 27

All houses make sounds at night: the icemaker filling up, the air-conditioning kicking on, the creaking of the stairs, and the chiming of the clock on the mantle. Rob Whedbee never heard any of those sounds as he slept, but there was something that disturbed his slumber. He wasn't sure if he was dreaming. He smelled cigarettes and something else: it was body odor.

His eyes adjusted to the faint light in the room. He was usually religious about completely shutting the blinds at night, but tonight, they were partially open, and the shards of light cast by the streetlight outside his bedroom were cutting through the dark enough to see it. A shadowy silhouette loomed over him with one arm raised.

What the…?

It was then Rob saw a long object clutched in the dark figure's raised hand, towards his neck. Instinctively, Rob threw up his arm in defense, just in time to deflect the oncoming blow. A searing pain shot through him as the deadly instrument filleted his earlobe and cut into the side of his throat. It was a large knife, Rob was sure, and he was gripped by a feeling he had rarely known: terror.

He's trying to kill me!

Most people feel safe and secure at night when they lock their doors and go to bed, but Rob was *not* safe. This was a life-and-death struggle, and he was at a disadvantage as this phantom still stood over him, poised to strike another blow. Rob struggled to raise up, grappling with his assailant, trying to get control of his wrists. He knew that if he failed to gain the upper hand, he was a dead man.

This was no dream; this was no nightmare. The man in the room with him was real as was the knife he was wielding. Rob was now wide awake, and he was furious. He was not going down easy, not at the hands of this specter in the night. He called out to Lisa, scared and screaming.

"Help! Lisa, someone is trying to kill me! Turn on the lights and call 911!"

No answer came.

Had this deadly fiend already killed her and maybe even Brittany?

This further fueled his efforts to gain control of the weapon. They were both panting from the struggle, and Rob could feel his own sweat seeping down his body. His mouth was filled with the taste of blood. This was hand-to-hand combat in a confined space, reminding Rob of his Golden Gloves days. The battle ebbed and flowed like a boxing match with each participant exerting a mighty effort and then backing off for a few seconds to regroup.

But where was Lisa? He called out again, but there was no answer. Rob fought harder to overcome his assailant and again was filled with the dread that maybe Lisa was already dead.

The cracked blinds allowed just enough light to seep into the room for Rob to get a better look at his opponent and make out his slight, wiry frame. Rob could not see his face because of the stocking mask he wore. The would-be killer was kneeling on top of him, still fighting to deliver a fatal blow when Rob finally got a good grip on one of the assassin's wrists, and they tumbled to the floor. He managed to come up behind his attacker, and although he had control of one of his wrists, the dark figure continued to swing the knife back and forth, pricking and nicking Rob in the torso and legs.

Rob knew he needed help. Once he finally had both the man's wrists restrained, he grabbed the phone from the nightstand. He pulled the phone's antenna out with his teeth and began to dial, but there was nothing. The phone was dead.

Suddenly, the right hand of his attacker broke his hold, and the knife was free. Rob dropped the phone and grabbed at the blade. His hand, slick with blood and sweat, slipped down the sharp edge of the blade. When his opponent realized this, he twisted the blade as hard as he could, slashing Rob's palm down to the bone. Rob's rage barely masked the extreme pain he was in as he tried with all his might to regain control of his assailant.

Suddenly, he was startled by the sound of a car driving over the drainage grate that ran across the width of the driveway. It made a clanging sound whenever anyone pulled in or out of the garage. Rob was seized by panic; this villain must have an accomplice. Rob was soon to learn he did.

Rob again called out for Lisa and felt a wave of relief wash over him as she finally appeared silhouetted in the doorway with an aluminum softball bat, raised and ready to swing.

"Lisa, get the lights! Call 911!"

Lisa did neither of these things, maintaining her stance. Then, in a cajoling way, she said, "Come on, Rob, let's get out of here. Let him go. Just let him go."

The next thing Rob heard shocked him. His attacker screamed out, "You've got to do it. Do it now!"

He knew that voice. His eyes were wide as the identity of his assailant hit him.

"Michael Frazier!"

Rob realized in that instant that Lisa was not there to help him. He was incensed, and the blatant sense of betrayal he felt carved much deeper than any of the physical wounds inflicted upon him. His opponent began to fight much harder. Their moans and groans punctuated the fight. It was now two against one, and Rob knew that to stay in that room would be his death sentence.

Mustering all his remaining energy, he picked up the would-be butcher and threw him hard, slamming him bodily into the corner of the room. Rob lunged for the bat, snatching it out of Lisa's hands as he fled the bedroom. Racing through the hallway, Rob, seized by alarm, could hear his attacker pursuing him as pictures fell from the walls and crashed to the floor.

He reached the kitchen and rushed through the door into the garage. He hit the garage door opener, turning on a bright overhead light and opening the garage door. He squared off, now in position to fight on equal terms.

When his attacker came through the door, still clutching his weapon, Rob was ready for him and raised the bat with every intention of bashing his brains in. But his hands and the bat were slick with sweat and blood, and the bat slipped out of his hands just before he could plant it into his foe's skull.

They were at a stalemate, but under the bright lights of the garage, Rob found himself staring into the beady eyes of Michael Frazier. Through his stocking mask, he stared back at Rob with his usual pinched expression. His *Phantom of the Opera* shirt glared at Rob, who would later conclude that it had been a critical part of Frazier's theatrical performance that bloody night. Realizing in his position, he was now the one at a disadvantage. Frazier turned and fled back in the house, locking the door behind him.

With lungs burning, heart pounding, and muscles fatigued and aching, Rob was seized by an adrenaline-fueled fury and overwhelming confusion. Without thinking, he kicked the kitchen door with his barefoot: another shock of pain. Rob felt the profuse sweat mixed with blood showering down from his face, splattering into puddles on the garage floor. He assessed his physical injuries, but no one could know the extent of the emotional damage that had so traumatized him that night and would for years to come.

It all made sense to him now; Aunt Martha was right about the affair, and now Lisa and Frazier were set on killing him. How could Lisa hate him so much that she wanted him dead? And if he was killed, poor Britt, he thought with dread, would surely end up in that "home." How would anyone be able to explain to Rob's eight-year-old son what his mother had done?

The violent bout seemed to have lasted an hour, although it had probably taken only about fifteen minutes or so for the vicious and destructive act to transpire. In his all-consuming exhaustion, Rob felt like he had just finished nine rounds in the ring.

Barefoot and barely dressed, Rob considered his next move. He knew he had to get help, so he rushed outside the garage and began beating on his gutters, screaming out to his neighbor and praying to be heard.

"Bill Shinn!" He clanged the bat against the gutters even harder this time. "Bill! Help! Someone's trying to kill me!"

Luckily, it had been a nice cool day in Knoxville, and Bill and his wife, Suzanne, had decided to leave their bedroom windows open. They had just finished watching a movie and were getting ready for bed when the racket started.

Bill turned to his wife and said, "I think that's Rob! Something must have happened with Brittany."

Bill went to the bedroom window that overlooked Rob's driveway and called out, "Rob, is that you?"

Rob was out of breath when he answered, "Bill, there is someone in my house, and he's trying to kill me!"

Bill wasted no time pulling on his pants and telling Suzanne to call 911.

"What should I say?" she asked.

"Tell them there is an intruder in the Whedbee house, and there may be some injuries."

When Bill came out, he was shocked to see Rob dressed in his undershorts and a tattered T-shirt soaked in blood. His face, neck, and hands were covered in blood.

"What the hell happened? Are you all right? Is there someone still in the house?"

"I don't know, but I'm going to try to cut them off at the back of the house. You stay here and keep watch."

Rob took off, still with barefeet, and disappeared around the back as Bill stood guard. Lisa finally drifted outside, still wearing her sexy nightie now stained with blood.

"Lisa, are you hurt? Where's Brittany?

"Bill, where's Rob? I've got to talk to Rob. He thinks I had something to do with this."

Bill thought maybe she was in shock as she wandered around like a pale ghostly apparition in the night. She kept murmuring over and over.

"Rob…"

Bill finally took her by the shoulders and walked her over to his house and told his wife to take care of her.

Rob had returned to the front of the house, and Bill asked him again, "What happened?"

"It was Michael Frazier, Bill. Michael Frazier tried to kill me!"

"Michael Frazier? Michael Frazier…from Trinity?" Bill asked in disbelieving shock.

"Michael Frazier!"

CHAPTER 28

At 1:18:53 a.m. of June 8, the radios at the Knox County Sherriff Department began to crackle. At one nineteen, two units were dispatched to 7500 Belfast Lane following an E-911 call reporting an intruder in the house.

A few minutes later, another call came in from a distressed woman screaming someone was trying to kill her next-door neighbor. Two more units were dispatched. By one thirty-nine, five units had arrived at the scene, and law enforcement milled in and out of the house.

Officer Gerald Weller was the first on the scene where he observed a chaotic situation at hand. He was advised that detectives were on the way. He saw a man in blue shorts with a blood-soaked T-shirt and assumed he was at least one of the victims, so Weller went over to talk to him to find out what exactly was going on and to see what kind of medical attention he might need. Rob was relieved to see him and told him his wife and her lover had tried to kill him. No one knew where the suspect or the wife were.

When the K-9 unit arrived, Rob went with them to again explore the woods behind his house. It was sizing up to be quite a night in Camelot.

CHAPTER 29

The room was dimly lit except for the flashes emanating from his TV screen. Kicked back in his comfy, brown leather recliner, he had drifted off somewhere between *NYPD Blue* and the talking heads on the eleven o'clock news. As he opened his eyes, he saw the mantle clock: 11:20 p.m.

He was on call, but it was a Tuesday night, and he really didn't expect much, if any, activity.

Yeah, he thought, *I could use a little shut-eye*, and he headed down the hallway to the bedroom.

He undressed, meticulously hanging up his khakis and tie and placing his glasses and watch on the nightstand beside the bed. He eased between the soft sheets and was asleep in no time.

It seemed as if only seconds had passed when the ringing phone jarred him from his sleep. In bright red numbers, the clock by the bed read one forty-two.

Damn, he thought as he answered. "Dan Stewart."

"Sorry, Dan," Sheila said from dispatch, "but we have a report of an armed intruder over in Karns. Do you want me to call Larry?"

"No, Sheila, I'll take care of it. Give me what you've got."

Dan made some notes; called his partner, Larry Johnson; and dressed—pants, shirt, tie, jacket, badge, and his gun.

What on earth could be going on in Camelot tonight? he wondered as he pulled out of the driveway. *Don't get many calls about trouble in that quiet neighborhood.*

Dan Stewart was a good detective, a very good detective. He had graduated from the Tennessee Law Enforcement Academy in '76 and picked up a bachelor's degree from Tusculum College. During his eighteen years with the Knox County Sheriff's Department, he had logged his hours as a patrol officer; and after six years of working the streets, he made detective in 1982. Believing law enforcement was a service profession, Dan took his work very seriously. Aware of the rapid changes occurring in law enforcement, Dan took continuing education classes to stay on top of advancements in the field.

Tall and lanky with rusty blond hair, Dan Stewart was an affable fellow who had an easy way of establishing rapport with people, especially suspects. Well-liked and well-respected by his peers, Dan was a savvy investigator, who excelled in assessing crime scenes and questioning "persons of interest." He also had a keen eye for spotting a lie, and he'd heard thousands of them over the years.

Larry Johnson was waiting in his driveway when Dan pulled up.

"Wake you up?" he asked Dan.

Dan nodded and said, "Yup."

Larry and Dan had been partners for more than a decade, and over the years, they had forged a strong bond of friendship. Larry had been an investigator for the Tennessee attorney general's office and had worked undercover for almost ten years. Dan had met him when he came to work for Knox County Sheriff's Department in '83. They began their partnership when Larry made lieutenant in the homicide division. Larry was a witty and cunning detective, and his investigative style complemented Dan's. They made a highly effective team, solving many cases together over the years.

There was no mistaking when Larry was in the building. Larry had a deep baritone voice that boomed across the squad room. He also had a great laugh and a smile that could almost always pick up your spirits. He was quite fond of beer, and when he was off duty, he could drink a boatload of Budweiser, enough, as they say, to drink an elephant under the table. People were drawn to the Silver Fox, as Larry was known. Men liked hanging with him, and women wanted to be with him. Dan always liked to kid that he got a front row seat for the "show." Work or play, Larry Johnson was just a great guy to have at your side.

Rubber turned on asphalt as Dan and Larry sped down Emory Road. As they made the turn onto Chartwell, they could already see the lights of several patrol cars; and when they made the right at Wickam, they saw the K-9 unit searching a wooded area behind the victim's house. The searchers' flashlights pierced through the dark as they combed the area. There was quite a commotion transpiring around 7500 Belfast Lane—deputies cordoning off the crime scene and patrol officers in and out of the house, taking pictures and collecting forensic evidence. They had already started taking statements from the neighbors.

Dan took it all in as he parked the car. He noticed Fred Ludwig, a sergeant with the department, standing in the driveway listening to a very animated man who was talking and gesturing with his hands. As he approached Fred, he observed that the man was about five feet ten inches and appeared to be in good physical condition. He had dark hair and mustache and was wearing a bloody T-shirt and gym shorts—obviously a victim.

"Howdy, Fred. What have we got?" Dan said, and then without waiting for an answer, he turned and introduced himself. "I'm Detective Dan Stewart, and I'll be the lead detective on your case."

Fred finished the introduction. "Dan, this is Robert Whedbee. He states that he was attacked by a man with a knife while he was sleeping."

"Thanks, Fred. I'll take it from here. We can compare notes later."

"Sure thing, Dan," the officer replied as he walked toward his patrol car.

Dan turned toward the man. Dan figured him to be in his early thirties.

"Mr. Whedbee, is it?"

"Rob. Rob Whedbee."

"Mr. Whedbee, I can plainly see you are still bleeding. Perhaps we should let the paramedics look at you."

"No," Rob firmly stated. "Let's get this thing going. I want to get the SOB!"

"Was anyone else in the house with you tonight?"

"My little girl's inside. She has Down syndrome. I think she slept through it, and my wife! She was part of it!"

Pulling out his pad and pen, Dan asked, "Part of what, Mr. Whedbee? What happened here tonight?"

Driven by adrenaline and a rage that seemed to grow exponentially, he answered, "Someone tried to kill me tonight, and I know who it was." He paused to wipe away some of the blood that was running down his neck and then continued, "It was Michael Frazier, the organist at our church, *and* my wife was involved."

"Mr. Whedbee, it would be helpful if you could walk me through the events of this evening. I'll need to get a formal statement from you."

Dan thought, *Whoa, nelly. This is going to be interesting.*

Rob led the detective into the house where uniformed officers were scurrying around, "bagging and tagging." As they walked toward the master bedroom, Dan could see where blood had streaked the walls of the hallway. Several pictures had been knocked to the floor. The master bedroom was in disarray, and it was obvious some type of struggle had taken place there. A tangle of bloody sheets and pillows was hanging off the bed. A lamp had been knocked to the floor, and the nightstand was askew. Dan also noted a bloody telephone off the hook, watching and listening as the distraught young man excitedly told him what had transpired during his struggle to save his life. Dan had a good sense for the trauma and terror Rob must have felt.

This guy was very lucky, Dan thought. "And you're sure you knew your attacker, Mr. Whedbee?" Dan asked as he continued to furiously scribble notes on his pad.

"As soon as I heard him speak, I knew it was Michael Frazier… I've known him for ten years. Hell, he and his wife have even vacationed with us at our cabin in Gatlinburg!"

"And what did you hear him say?"

Rob took a deep breath. "Well, once I realized I was being attacked, I kept calling for my wife. I began to worry that maybe she was already dead. Still I kept calling for her to turn on the lights and call 911. I had the guy by the wrists but couldn't get control of the knife. I tried to hold onto both his wrists with one hand so I could dial 911 on the bedside phone, but the line was dead. He had already cut my ear and my throat, and as I tried to get control of both his wrists, my hand slipped down on the knife blade, which he turned around in my hand, slicing my palm and cutting the hell out of my thumb. Then out of nowhere Lisa, my wife, appeared in the bedroom doorway clutching a softball bat. At first, I was relieved, but then I heard him say, 'You've got to do it. Do it now!' I immediately knew it was Frazier's voice and that it was the two of them against me. I had to get out of that room. I used all my strength and threw the bastard into the corner and took off. I grabbed the bat from my wife on my way out of the room."

The two men walked back into the hallway, and Rob went on recounting the events of the night.

"I was running toward the kitchen door on the other side of the house, but I could hear him chasing me."

Along with the bloody marks along the hallway walls, there was a perfect bloody handprint on the kitchen door.

"You exited the house here?"

Dan stopped writing and took a good look around the garage. A black Jimmy and a gold Corvette took up much of the space, leaving little room for combat.

"What happened next, Rob?"

"He followed me into the garage with the knife. The lights were on, and I could see him. I could tell it was him even with the mask on. In the light, I could clearly see it *was* Michael Frazier!"

"Did the two of you engage at that point?"

"Well," Rob explained, "I was ready to take a good swing at him with the bat, but my hands were slick from all the blood, and the bat slipped. When I got control of it again, he had gone back in the house and locked the door behind him. I'm locked out, no phone, and barely dressed, and my baby girl was still in the house. I had to find a way to get some help. That's when I started banging on my front gutters, yelling to my next-door neighbor, 'Someone's trying to kill me!'"

An embankment and a row of trees along the driveways separated the two houses. They walked down the path to get a better look at the house next door.

"And Mr. Shinn responded?"

"Yes, he came out to help me. I wasn't sure if Frazier was still in the house, but I left Bill out front standing guard, and I went around back to try and cut him off. When the first patrol car came by, they picked me up and took over the search."

"What about your wife, Mr. Whedbee? Where was she during all of this?"

Mrs. Whedbee had been conspicuously absent since Dan had arrived.

With a disgusted laugh, Rob said, "Oh yeah, she came outside and kept coming over to me, saying, 'Oh, Rob, you're hurt. Let me help you.' She tried to put her arms around me, but I told her to get away from me. I knew what was going on."

"And you're certain your wife was involved?"

"Absolutely."

"Have there been marital problems, Mr. Whedbee?"

Dan had noticed many large professional family photographs while he was in the house. They looked like the perfect family—good-looking mother and father and two beautiful kids.

You never know what lies behind appearances.

"Problems?" Rob said, rubbing his forehead. "Yeah, there have been problems ever since our little girl was born. My wife wanted to put her in a facility, but I always refused. No way was I going to put my little girl in some home. Of course, it's been hard, but I am determined that I will love and take care of Britt as long as I am able. I love my little girl, and she loves me."

Rob continued, "My wife was interviewed by Frazier a little over a year ago for a newspaper article about how hard it is to raise a disabled child. He made her out to be a saint when it was me and the grandparents raising the kids. But that was okay. I figured she just wanted her fifteen minutes of fame. Then she got involved with the choir at Trinity Methodist. Sometimes, she wouldn't be home until after eleven, and I did think that was a little late for choir practice.

Even Lisa's mother asked me several times, when she was babysitting, if I didn't wonder where Lisa was so late. Quite frankly, things had gotten so bad between us. I was actually relieved when she was gone." He paused. "Is any of this helpful? I'm not sure how much information you really need," Rob asked.

"It all has direct bearing on the case," Dan replied, nodding. "Go on."

"Last October, I think it was…my aunt called me and suggested Lisa and Michael were seeing each other."

"Your aunt?"

"Yes, Martha Walker. She works at the same school where Frazier's wife works, and Mrs. Frazier had confided in my aunt that she had reason to believe Michael was having an affair with some blonde. Based on several strange conversations Lisa had had with my aunt, Martha thought there was a good chance Lisa was Michael's mistress. To be honest, it almost cracked me up at the thought, but I did confront Lisa about it. She acted shocked and told me she could do a lot better than Michael Frazier. I feel like a real idiot," Rob went on. "I thought maybe there was something going on between them, but I wanted to believe her."

About that time, Paul Hughes, another officer on the scene, tapped Dan on the shoulder and said, "Boss is here."

"Great," Dan said. "I'll catch up with him in a little while. I need to talk to the wife and neighbors."

Dan turned back to Rob and said, "You've been very helpful, Mr. Whedbee. I'll probably need to talk with you again, but why don't you let the medics look at you? Go check on your daughter again, and try to find a place where you can sit down and catch your breath."

Rob nodded at Dan and said, "Thanks. I'll be close by if you need me."

"Is there anything I can do for you right now?" Dan asked.

"Yeah…catch the bastard."

"Don't worry, Mr. Whedbee." Dan smiled at Rob, and with absolute confidence, he said, "We'll get the S.O.B."

The Sunsphere, built for the 1982 World's Fair
still accentuates the Knoxville Skyline.

Rob Whedbee in elementary school.

Rob, at 16.

Lisa Outlaw's senior picture.

Rob excelled as a Golden Gloves boxer.

Rob competes in the 1980 Teenage National Power Lifting Championship while his father, Lloyd watches in the background in Chicago.

At 19, Rob was an accomplished power lifter.

Lisa and Rob enjoying the early days of their relationship.

Lisa and Rob attended Lisa's prom.

Lisa Outlaw became Mrs. Robert Whedbee
on June 12, 1982.

Rob holds his new baby girl,
Brittany Alice Whedbee.

Miss Britt celebrates her first Christmas.

Brittany learns to walk before the age of two.

Brittany makes a beautiful little angel
in the church Christmas pageant.

Big brother, Justin,
was always there for his baby sister.

Justin and Brittany were never far apart.

Britt loved her Pops, Lloyd Whedbee.

After her mother's departure from Rochester,
Britt turns 2 at the Mayo Clinic.

Justin and Rob share their love of fishing.

The "perfect family" portrait.

Lloyd and Joyce Whedbee celebrated
more than sixty years together.

7500 Belfast, the Whedbee's home which
would later become a crime scene.

Where It All Started, Trinity Methodist Church, 5615 Western Avenue

Where They Got It On, 4127D Brendon Park

Top: Trinity United Methodist Church where he fell in love
with Lisa Whebee. Michael Frazier testified. Bottom: The
apartment Frazier rented for his and Lisa's rendezvous.

Lisa posing for a Glamour Shot for her lover,
Michael Frazier.

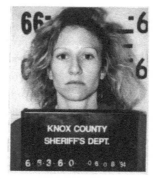

Lisa Outlaw Whedbee poses for her mug shot.

Arrested on attempted murder, Michael David
Frazier's mug shot was taken.

Frazier was most proud of the shirt he wore
when he tried to kill Rob.

The bat and knife used in the attempt on
Rob's life were taken as evidence.

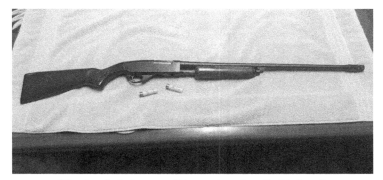

The loaded shotgun Lisa pointed at Rob's head.

Exact spot where attack occurred.

Flanked by her attorneys, Lisa Whedbee arrives
at court for her pre-trial hearing.

Lead detective, Dan Stewart, played a vital role investigating
the attempted murder of Rob Whedbee.

Judge Richard Baumgartner presides over
Tennessee v. Michael Frazier.

Brutalized on the stand by the defense, Robert Whedbee
demonstrates the terrifying sight he awoke to on June 8, 1994.

Greg Isaacs displays the award-winning article
his client wrote about Lisa Whedbee.

Well-coached by his attorney, Michael Frazier
testifies with a multitude of lies.

Frazier anxiously awaits the
return of the verdict.

Lisa Whedbee Weatherly prepares to make
her plea and receive her sentence.

IN THE CRIMINAL/CIRCUIT COURT OF KNOX COUNTY, TENNESSEE

Case Number: 55985   Count # 3RD
Judicial District Sixth Judicial Division I

Attorney for the State   Randall E. Nichols
Counsel for Defendant T. DILLARD & D. ELDRIDGE
☒ Retained;   ☐ Appointed;   ☐ Public Defender

State of Tennessee
vs.
Defendant LISA O. WHEDBEE, ALIAS
Date of Birth _____ Sex F   Race W
From Indictment # 55985   Warrant # 944081

Alias _____
SSN ___ - __ - ____
TDOC # _____

FILED
BY MARTHA PHILLIPS, CLERK

JUN 2 4 1996

JUDGMENT

KNOX COUNTY CRIMINAL COURT
KNOXVILLE, TN

Comes the District Attorney General for the State and the defendant with counsel of record for entry of judgment.
On the 24TH day of JUNE , 19 96 the defendant:

☒ pled guilty

Is found:
☐ guilty   ☐ not guilty
☐ jury verdict   ☐ not guilty by reason of insanity
☐ bench trial
☐ nolo contendere

Indictment: Class (circle one): 1st (A) B C D E ☒ Felony ☐ Misdemeanor
Offense ATT. MURDER & CONSP. TO COMMIT 1ST DEG. MURDER
Amended Charge SOL. TO COMMIT 2ND DEG. MURDER
Offense date 06 / , 94 County KNOX
Conviction offense SOLICITATION TO COM. 2ND DEG. MURDER
TCA 39-12-102 & 39-13-210   Sentence imposed date 06 , 24 , 96
Conviction class (circle one): 1st A B (C) D E   ☒ Felony ☐ Misdemeanor

After considering the evidence, the entire record, and all factors in T.C.A. Title 40, Chapter 35, all of which are incorporated by reference herein, the Court's findings and rulings are:

☒ Sentence Reform Act of 1989
☐ Mitigated 20%
☐ Mitigated 30%
☒ Standard 30% Range 1
☐ Multiple 35% Range 2
☐ Persistent 45% Range 3
☐ Career 60%   ☐ Multiple Rapist
☐ 1st Degree Murder   ☐ Child Rapist

☐ Pre 1982 Sentence: _____
☐ 1st Degree Murder
☐ Sentence Reform Act of 1982
☐ 20% Range 1
☐ 30% Range 1
☐ 35% Range 2
☐ 40% Range 2
☐ 1st Degree Murder

Concurrent with:

Consecutive to:

Sentenced to: Sentence Length:
☒ TDOC   4 Years ___ Months ___ Days ___ Life   ☐ Death
☐ Regional Workhouse   ___ Years ___ Months ___ Days
☒ County Jail   1 Years ___ Months ___ Days ___ Hours ___ Week-ends ___ Periodic: (_____)
___% min. svc. prior to program or work release 100 % min. svc. prior to release (Misdemeanor only)
☐ Workhouse   ___ Years ___ Months ___ Days ___ Hours ___ Week-ends ___ Periodic: (_____)
___% min. svc. prior to program or work release ___% min. svc. prior to release (Misdemeanor only)
☐ Work Release   ___ Years ___ Months ___ Days ___ Hours ___ Week-ends
☒ Probation   3 Years ___ Months ___ Days Effective: 06/24/97
☐ Community Based Alternative ___ Years ___ Months ___ Days ___ Hours ___ Week-ends
Specify: _____

Pretrial Jail Credit Period: from __/__/__ to __/__/__ from __/__/__ to __/__/__ or Number of Days: _____

Court Ordered Fees and Fines:
$ 50.00   Criminal Injuries
  Compensation Fund
$ _____ Supervision
$ _____ Child Support
$ 740.12 Court Costs
$ _____ T.B.I.F.
$ _____ FINE ASSESSED

Restitution:
Victim's Name _____
Address _____
Total Amount $ _____ $ _____ per month
☐ Unpaid Community Service ___ Hours, ___ Days, ___ Weeks, ___ Months

☒ The defendant having been found guilty is rendered infamous.

Special Conditions:
ON RECOMMENDATION OF THE ATTORNEY GENERAL AND BY AUTHORITY OF T.C.A. 40-35-314 THE DEFENDANT SHALL SERVE 1 YEAR IN THE KNOX COUNTY JAIL (100%) AND THE BALANCE OF THIS SENTENCE IS HEREBY SUSPENDED ON PAYMENT OF COSTS AND THE

Lisa is convicted of conspiracy to commit second-degree murder.

Grandparents, Joyce and Lloyd Whedbee share
a Christmas morning with Miss Britt.

Joyce and Britt have fun looking through pictures.

Still as close as ever, Justin and Britt talk about their day.

Britt loves Dad and the feeling is mutual!

Rob and the kids in 2011.

Justin Whedbee follows in his dad's footsteps and does very well.

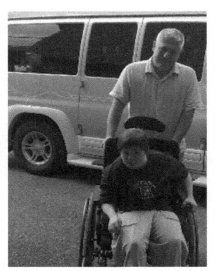

Rob and Miss Britt return from an outing.

CHAPTER 30

Funny thing about a crime scene—protocol and order can easily be derailed by the arrival of manic media and curious neighbors crowding around curious to know what's going on. Knoxville Sheriff Tim Hutchison was on the scene and was making his presence known. The first responders were still there, and seven or eight various law enforcement officials were still bustling about.

Dan saw the crime reporter for the *Knoxville News Sentinel* pull up, and right behind him, it was a satellite truck for one of the local news stations. More were sure to show up, so Dan called Gerald Weller, the first officer on the scene, to run interference between the media and the victims.

"And no one crosses the crime tape without authorization!" Dan shouted to Officer Weller.

Dan saw Sheriff Hutchison and Mr. Whedbee were sitting in lawn chairs right inside of the garage behind where the Corvette was parked. Tim was obviously trying to talk Rob down, and one of the paramedics was unsuccessfully trying to administer first aid to him. They had managed to convince him to at least wrap a towel, now totally blood soaked, around his hand. They would later find that Frazier had completely severed his tendon and radial artery, split his earlobe in two, and covered him with a smattering of other superficial, yet painful, nicks and bruises.

Rob was a man of order and routine, and this mass pandemonium unfolding around him was making his anger and anxiety escalate.

Officer Hughes caught up with Dan and asked, "So what do you think?"

Also annoyed by the chaos, Dan answered, "I'm not sure what to think just yet...and where the hell is the wife anyway?"

"I believe she's still asleep on the neighbor's couch..."

"Sleeping?" Dan shouted in disbelief. "Her husband was almost killed, and her baby girl is still in the house, and she's *sleeping*? Go wake her up, and get her out here...sleeping? You've absolutely got to be kidding me."

Dan stood there shaking his head. Paul returned with Mrs. Whedbee in tow. She looked pale and shaken and had a "little girl lost" look in her eyes.

"Dan Stewart, Mrs. Whedbee. I'm going to need to talk with you about the events of the night."

She spoke in a tiny, barely audible voice you might expect from a five-year-old. It grated on Dan's nerves.

"I...I...just don't know what's happening. I want to talk to my husband, and I need to make sure my little girl is all right."

"Your husband is talking with the sheriff, and your little girl is still asleep in the house."

Dan turned to Paul and said, "Take Mrs. Whedbee down to one of the squad cars and put her in the back."

He wanted to give her plenty of time to "stew and brew," and he let her sit out there for more than twenty minutes before he finally went down to talk with her.

By nature, Dan was an empathetic person. He had learned over time that sometimes, a little empathy expedites a suspect's willingness to talk. He was trying to stay objective, but his gut was telling him not to trust this one. Lisa Whedbee would not be getting much empathy from Detective Dan Stewart.

As he got in the car, Lisa was crying and saying over and over, "Rob...Brittany...I need to see them."

Despite her cries, her worries about them hadn't seemed to keep her from a nice nap on her neighbor's couch. It was 3:20 a.m. when he started recording his interview.

"Lisa, I have explained a standard rights waiver with you, is that correct?"

"Yes, sir."

Damn that baby voice, Dan wanted to strangle her, but he knew he needed to be objective. He reconfirmed her understanding of her rights, and she agreed to talk to him without representation. With her sad eyes and her little voice, Lisa began to tell him her version of the night's event.

"I went to bed about ten thirty and had just drifted off when Rob got in bed and started being 'romantic.'"

"So you and your husband made love?"

"Yes," she said. "And after that, Rob fell asleep and began to snore. I know from experience I would not be able to sleep with him snoring. I got on the couch in the family room, and I guess I had been asleep about an hour when I heard Rob start yelling. It startled me because it was a…a funny voice I didn't recognize, but it was Robert.

"I started down the hall toward the bedroom, and I could hear him struggling and fighting…I just…I got real…you know, scared. I didn't know what to do, but I knew there was a bat in my little boy's toy chest, so I went and got it. When I got back to the bedroom, I could see Rob had someone pinned down on the bed, and I told him we needed to get out of the house. I grabbed him by the arm and tried to lead him out, and I noticed he was getting blood all over me. I said, 'Rob, you're bleeding. Let him go, and let's get out of here.' He got up and took off down the hall toward the kitchen. I just didn't know what to do. I was scared and worried about Rob and my little girl. I went up to Bill, our neighbor, and begged him to go get Brittany who has Down syndrome."

"What did Mr. Shinn do?"

"He took me over to his house. I remember I was shaking really bad…I don't know if it was because I was cold or just so scared."

Dan watched her closely as she told her story. Her eyes were teary and darted around, avoiding eye contact with Dan. Every few seconds, she would bury her face in her hands, but Dan pushed her on.

"Lisa, did you see the other person your husband was fighting with?"

"I never saw. I saw, you know, like a dark shadow."

"Do you have any idea who the person was in your house tonight?"

It was then she looked him straight in the eyes and said, "No. I do not know who the person was. I never saw the person…you know with the lights, I mean, we never turned them on."

Dan thought to himself, *Why hadn't she turned on the lights or called 911?* But he didn't ask. He would save that question for later.

Lisa was shivering and pulled up the blanket her neighbor's wife had given her. The tape was recording their conversation, but at the moment, Dan was more focused on her body language. She was still shaking and almost—Dan searched for the right word—squirming. That's it: she was squirming.

Dan continued to ask questions, and she continued to answer in her meek and sorrowful voice. So far, it was sort of a humdrum interview until he asked her about the phone being off the hook in her son's bedroom.

Lisa responded, "This is going to sound silly…uh…well… sometimes when I have the pig in the house…"

Dan shook his head. *Had she said "pig"?*

"What I mean is sometimes, the pig will root around and knock the phone off the hook."

Dan still couldn't believe what he was hearing.

"Are you talking about a pet pig?"

"Yes, sir."

A pet pig, Dan had finally heard it all. The woman had a pig as a pet. It was time to get serious, and Dan leaned closer to her and asked, "Do you know a Michael Frazier?"

It was barely noticeable, but she flinched.

"Yes, uh…he goes to our church. He plays the organ."

Going in for the kill, Dan asked her, "Have you talked with him or seen him tonight?"

Her eyes turned cold and said, "No."

"Have you ever had a relationship outside your marriage with Mr. Frazier?"

"No," she responded defensively. "I mean, you know, we're friends. I'm friends with him and his wife."

Dan had her where he wanted her and decided to let her sit there by herself for a little while longer.

"I think we've covered the high points of tonight's events, Mrs. Whedbee. I need to check on a few things, and then I'll have more questions for you. Maybe while you wait here, you'll think of other details that would be helpful."

"That's fine, but can I see my husband? I really need to talk with him."

"We'll see. You just sit tight for the time being, and I'll be back in a little while."

She started to protest and was getting teary-eyed again, but Dan shut the car door and went back up to the house.

No one ever knew what Lisa was thinking as she sat there in the dark, replaying the answers she had given. And who would believe sweet and innocent Lisa Whedbee could be potentially responsible for one man's death, and possibly two more murders? It didn't matter to her one bit what impact the events of that night would have on other people. She was only worried about herself. Besides that, she just didn't care.

CHAPTER 31

After his interview with Mrs. Whedbee, Dan returned to the garage where Mr. Whedbee was still sitting with Sheriff Hutchison.

Shaking his head, Dan said, "Boss, I think she's lying. I'm going to let her stew for a little bit and then bring her in the house and give it another go."

The sheriff commented, "If that's what your gut is saying, then it probably is a pack of lies. See what else you can get out of her."

"Oh, and Mr. Whedbee? She wants to talk to you."

"I have nothing to say to her. In fact, I don't want her near me. She was the one behind what happened tonight," Rob went on. "I'll be filing for divorce today."

It was almost five o'clock in the morning when Officer Gerald Weller went down to get Mrs. Whedbee out of the patrol car. He brought her up to the house and led her to the living room where Rob, Dan Stewart, and Officer Paul Hughes were situated, waiting to observe Dan's second interview.

"Lisa, come on in and have a seat," Dan said, motioning her, and once again started the tape recorder.

She must have felt like a bug under a microscope. There was blood on her arms and on her nightgown, and she was shaking. Her hair looked something akin to Medusa's serpents as her head drooped down toward her chest. She avoided eye contact with anyone in the room.

Dan began, "Lisa, tell me what happened here at your house tonight, as far as the incidents we've been discussing, and tell me the truth."

Lisa started speaking softly, "We came into the house…"

"Mrs. Whedbee, please speak up," Dan requested.

"We came into the house about seven o'clock, and I went to give Brittany a bath. He went downstairs."

"Tell me who he is."

"Michael went downstairs."

"Michael, who?"

Lisa answered but kept her head down, afraid she might make eye contact with Rob.

"Frazier."

"Why was Michael Frazier here?" Dan asked.

"To help me, he said."

"Did you know what he was going to do?"

"I did not know what his intentions were," Lisa stated.

"Tell me how Michael Frazier came into the house."

"Through the kitchen door."

"Did he come in with you?"

"I was here."

Lisa was trying her best to give them a statement that might at least fairly resemble the truth. She'd changed her story again, and Dan had no illusions that he might get the whole truth.

"Okay. Where did he go when he came in?"

"Downstairs," Lisa answered.

"Tell me why Michael came over here? You said earlier he was going to help you. What was he going to help you do?"

Tearing up again, Lisa went on.

"He was convinced that Rob was gonna hurt or kill me, and he didn't want him to, so he was going to help me."

"What did, uh, Michael…"

Lisa interrupted Dan to say, "And I don't know *how* or *what*."

"What did Michael tell you he was going to do?"

"He never really talked about it in detail. I don't know…"

"What, what…" Dan encouraged her to go on.

"His intentions," she finished.

The people in the room looked at each other with skepticism.

Dan went on and said, "I understand. What exactly *did* he tell you? You said earlier that he made a statement about Robert…something he was gonna do."

"He was just going to, you know…I don't remember exactly what he said. The truth is I don't remember."

Dan wasn't buying it and continued to prod her for some truth.

"Let me refresh your memory," Dan began. "You've told me that Michael Frazier was going to take care of your husband. Do you remember telling me that?"

Like a broken record, she repeated, "Take care of the matter, I mean." Lisa paused for several seconds and said again, "Take care of the matter. But as far as what and how, we did not discuss that."

"So tell me about the events after Michael came in and went downstairs. What did you do here in the house?"

Finally, it was a question Lisa could answer truthfully.

"I took Brittany and gave her a bath, put on her pajamas, and then took a shower while she waited for me. I made up her bed, folded the sheets down, and then we got in. We were reading books, and the whole time, she kept calling for Da-Da because she hadn't seen Rob in two days. After that, he came in and started playing with Brittany. I did some laundry. I did some computer work for Rob. I painted my fingernails and then went to bed."

"What time did Rob come home tonight?"

"He got home probably around eight twenty."

"What time did you go to bed?"

"It was ten thirty."

Dan went on and said, "You said you went to bed with your husband and you made love and then went to sleep on the couch in the den?"

"Yes, I came in here because he started snoring. It was about eleven thirty. That's all I know."

"And, uh, you subsequently went to sleep on the couch?" Dan asked.

"Well, I was sitting up in the corner 'cause my neck was hurting again. Rob knows I've been having a neck problem. I came in here because he was snoring," she said again.

"What woke you from your sleep?"

"Rob was screaming, calling for me. At first, I could hear him saying, 'Lisa, quit it. What are you doing to me? Stop it!'"

"These other things you've told me in the previous statement, that's what happened?"

Lisa stared Dan hard in the eyes, "That's *exactly* what happened after that. Nothing, nothing changed. That's the truth."

From across the room, Rob sat, shaking his head, but remained silent. As he listened, he wondered what her story would have been had he not survived the murder attempt. He felt sure that Lisa would have used the bat to also kill Frazier, leaving her to play the pitiful victim. Her story would have been very believable and surely would have evoked an outpouring of sympathy. *An intruder had slaughtered her husband, and she, in self-defense, was able to kill him.*

Not satisfied that he had what he needed, Dan went on with a few more questions.

"Okay, Mrs. Whedbee, tell me about when you and Michael Frazier talked about this…about something happening."

"It was after that Sunday. I don't know the exact date."

"Tell me about the Sunday you are referring to."

"It was after that Sunday, another thing that, you know, just got out of hand. Rob said I was going to shoot him."

The four men in the room all sat up when they heard her response.

Lisa went on and said, "It was a Sunday afternoon. He walked downstairs and said I had a shotgun aimed at him. He kept saying it was loaded."

Rob remembered that Sunday afternoon, and the shotgun *had* been loaded. It was a little bit more than a situation that just got out of hand.

"After that incident, you and Michael Frazier talked about this one tonight? The thing that happened tonight?"

Nodding her head, Lisa answered, "Yes."

"Did you talk in any specific terms about it?"

"No. Just that Michael was afraid Rob was going to kill me. He just…you know."

Dan, growing more and more suspicious, asked, "And you don't know what Frazier was going to do in this house tonight? He didn't tell you?"

"No."

"Anything else you want to tell me about the incident tonight?"

"I told you every…everything."

"Is this the truth?" Dan asked.

"Yes," Lisa answered.

When Lisa had finished telling her tale, Dan stood up to face her.

"Mrs. Whedbee, I have read your Miranda rights several times, would you agree?"

Lisa nodded with tear-filled eyes.

"And you understand these rights as I have read them to you?"

Lisa nodded again and began to cry.

"At this time, Mrs. Whedbee, I am arresting you for the attempted first-degree murder and solicitation to commit the murder of your husband," Dan informed her.

Lisa immediately started sobbing and crying out for Rob. Rob, thoroughly disgusted by this time, walked out of the room but watched as they cuffed her. Officer Weller walked her out to the patrol car and assisted getting her in the back. Lisa Whedbee, with smeared makeup, wild hair, and a nightgown covered in blood, was taken downtown to be fingerprinted. Her picture, far from the glamour shots she was so proud of, looked like forty miles of bad road.

CHAPTER 32

It was about six o'clock in the morning when the ringing phone sliced through the silence, rousing Lloyd and Joyce Whedbee from their slumber. Joyce sat up in bed, already alarmed. She knew if the phone was ringing at this hour, it couldn't be good news. Joyce's mind immediately went to Brittany. They'd been through many emergency calls related to her chronic health issues. Lloyd picked up the phone and began to listen, and Joyce watched his face go pale and then contort in concern and disbelief, and she wasn't quite sure, but it looked like anger.

When Lloyd finally spoke, his first words to the caller were "that bitch." Lloyd *never* used profanity, and Joyce thought maybe she had misunderstood him. Anxiety consumed her as she listened to her husband, waiting patiently to find out what was going on, but she never could have prepared herself for what he told her when he hung up the phone.

"Is it Brittany?" she asked.

Lloyd shook his head, sitting back down on the edge of the bed.

"Lisa and Michael Frazier tried to kill Rob tonight."

Stunned in disbelief, Joyce felt as if she had been kicked in the gut.

"Is Rob okay? What happened? What do we need to do?"

She started to get dressed as she began to process what her husband was telling her. Rob was at the hospital. Frazier had attacked him with a butcher knife. If Rob hadn't awakened, he would probably be headed to the morgue instead of the hospital. And Lisa was in on it too.

Joyce tried to get her mind around what Lloyd was telling her but still found it hard to fathom.

"Rob wants you to go take care of Brittany until he can get back home, and I need to make some calls," Lloyd told her. "You know," Lloyd continued, "I've had a bad feeling about that girl for a long time, but I never would have believed she was capable of something like this."

Driving to Rob's house, Joyce began to think about something strange that had happened the previous afternoon. Lisa and the kids, Justin and Brittany, had come over for a swim and some dinner. Justin was going to spend the night with them, and she assumed Brittany would stay as well. She and Lloyd loved having the grandkids over, and Lisa was always relieved to shed her maternal role and let them stay, especially Brittany.

That was not the case this time. Lloyd and Joyce tried to convince her to leave Brittany as well, but Lisa was adamant that Brittany had to go home with her.

Lloyd said, "Come on, Lisa, let her stay."

In an ugly tone, she told her father-in-law, "Put her in the car right now! She's going home with me."

As he listened to the adults, eight-year-old Justin was getting more and more upset and begged his mom to let "Little Toot," as he liked to call her, stay with him. When she repeatedly refused, Justin made up his mind that he would go home as well and climbed in the back seat of Lisa's car. Lisa ordered him out of the car, and after much hesitation, he obeyed. By this time, he was crying and still pleading with his mom. As Lisa began to back out of the driveway, Justin grabbed on to the door handle as if he could get his mom to stop. It was a truly pitiful sight to see a little boy crying and holding tight to the car and running down the driveway until Lisa finally pulled away. All Justin could do was cry as he watched his mom disappear down the road.

Lloyd and Joyce had both commented to each other about how strange the incident was. In Joyce's opinion, Lisa usually couldn't get rid of Brittany quick enough. Even after four years, she had never really bonded with her child with severe disabilities and blamed her for ruining her perfect world.

She continued to reflect on the strange incident. She wondered, *Did Justin know something? He was always protective of his little sister. Had he sensed something? And if Lisa was planning on killing Rob that night, why was it so important that Brittany be there?*

A horrific thought came to her, and her blood ran cold. Maybe Lisa had also planned to get rid of Brittany. Joyce felt like she was going to vomit. She rolled down the window to get some air, still reeling as the vile thought circled through her brain. She could not wait to hold her granddaughter and to see her son. Joyce Whedbee was a strong, take charge woman, and she would do whatever she could to help her family get through this dreadful nightmare.

The first shafts of light were beginning to stretch across the sky when Joyce pulled into Rob's driveway. Rob's neighbor, Bill, met her at the door.

"Where's Brittany?" she asked.

Bill replied that she was still sound asleep in her room.

"As a matter of fact," Bill began, "I can't believe she slept through the whole thing. Rob told me there was a lot of screaming and banging, and then of course, there were all the sirens and the deputies and investigators moving around the house collecting evidence. As you can imagine, it's been a pretty bizarre night."

Joyce hurried to Brittany's room and reached down to feel her head and stroke her soft hair. She was warm and breathing slowly, and for a moment, Joyce was relieved. That was her precious granddaughter, and no one better ever try to harm her.

Bill led Joyce to the scene of the crime as he told her what he knew about the events of the night. Blood streaked the sheets on the bed, and there was more blood on the carpet and walls. The room was in disarray, and it was obvious there had been a struggle. There was blood on the walls of the hallway, and pictures were either knocked down or askew. The door to the garage revealed bloody handprints on both sides.

"How badly was Rob hurt? There's so much blood."

Joyce could not believe her eyes.

"I don't think he sustained any critical injuries. When Frazier first tried to stab him, Rob was able to deflect the knife. It cut his neck and took a chunk out of his ear. He also got a bad cut on his hand and thumb, but I think Rob was able to overpower him. He was nicked up badly, but Frazier never delivered any serious blows."

"I still can't believe it was Michael Frazier. Are you sure it was him?"

"I thought for sure, Rob must be mistaken," Bill exclaimed. "And then Lisa was acting whacko, following me around saying Rob thought she had something to do with this. The cops just arrested her."

"Well, I'm going to go check on Brittany again," Joyce said. "I probably ought to wake her up and take her to my house. Thank you for all you have done, Bill. You're a good neighbor."

"I'm just glad I heard Rob. I'll hang around for a while, just in case anything else comes up. Call me if you need anything."

Morning light was filtering through the blinds in Brittany's room, and Joyce could clearly see she was still asleep. Joyce gently shook her, softly calling her name. After several minutes without response, Joyce felt a growing fear. She turned on the light and tried to get Brittany upright in the bed.

"Brittany," she said loudly. "It's time to wake up."

The child remained unresponsive. Her eyes were heavily matted, and her body was lax. Joyce's worry escalated. Not wanting to leave the child alone, Joyce called for Bill to bring her some warm washcloths, which she gently rubbed across Britt's eyes, trying to remove some of the glue-like matting. She continued to talk to Brittany as she stroked her face and neck with the warm cloths.

"Please, please wake up, Brittany," she said over and over, holding the child up and rocking her back and forth.

Tortuous minutes passed by, but Joyce never stopped working on Brittany, and her heart leaped when she felt Brittany's arm move. Soon she began to open her eyes, looking at her grandmother, dazed and disoriented. Joyce glanced at the clock and realized she had been trying to wake her for more than an hour. She picked up the small girl and hugged her, uttering a silent prayer of thanks. Joyce bundled her up and headed to her car to take her home with her, to keep her safe.

Lisa Whedbee, liar, adulteress, and attempted murderess, would never hold her baby girl again, and sadly, she would never even ask to. She vanished from both of her children's lives. The perfect family she had longed for was weighing her down. She finally found her ticket out of the Whedbee family and into the county jail.

Even with one alleged assailant apprehended, there was still another guilty party to track down.

CHAPTER 33

After his confrontation with Rob in the garage, Frazier ran back into the house. He knew his knife was no match for a bat. He gave Lisa the knife and rushed out the downstairs door, running for the woods at the back of the Whedbees' lot. There, he tossed the ripped and bloody latex gloves he had been wearing. His approximate time of flight was 1:39 a.m.

Frazier was a shaken man, to say the least. He was seized by rapid-fire heart palpitations, and his lungs felt as if they had been crushed during the struggle with Rob. He knew he was caught and most likely, Lisa too. Worst of all, he had failed Lisa, and now they would both have to pay. He berated himself for his inadequacy. It had sounded so simple when he and Lisa had discussed it. They had so much to gain, if only he had been successful in his endeavor to end Rob's life. Now, all was lost. Michael Frazier would not be a freeman for long.

He knew they were already searching for him. As he crossed over Emory Road, he could hear the sirens in the distance. There would be cops with flashlights, spotlights, and K-9 units trying to sniff out his trail. He had to put as much distance as possible between him and 7500 Belfast.

No one knows for sure what Michael did during the four and a half hours before he was arrested. Lisa had picked him up at his apartment Tuesday night, so he did not have his car, but could another person have been waiting for him in one of the neighborhoods off West Emory? Lisa's best friend Tammy, whom she had known since childhood, would have done anything for her. Could she have also been an accomplice?

Perhaps he made the 7.74-mile trek to the apartment on Grayland Drive he had rented for Lisa and himself. Being a heavy smoker, it most likely would have taken him close to two hours to reach the apartment. From there, he would have only had a little less than two miles to his apartment on Jenny Cook Circle that he shared with his wife, a distance he could probably cover in twenty to thirty minutes.

However, Michael actually made the full journey from the Whedbee's home to Jenny Cook Circle; Lieutenant Fred Ludwig and Sergeant Larry Moore were waiting for him when he walked up through the apartment parking lot at approximately 6:15 a.m. Several news crews were also there, hoping to get a statement, some pictures, and footage of the arrest. Seeing them was no surprise, but Michael made a feeble attempt to joke.

"Well, don't tell me my wife has filed another complaint against me."

Fred Ludwig was not amused by Michael's lame humor and told Michael to raise his hands while Larry Moore frisked him.

"Michael Frazier, you are under arrest for the attempted murder of Rob Whedbee," Fred said, proceeding to Mirandize him as he cuffed him.

Ravenous reporters and camera crews clamored around, trying to get some word from Michael. They reveled in getting pictures of him being cuffed and put into the back seat of the police cruiser. Michael covered his face as the cruiser pulled away. He had lost everything, but the thing he mourned the most was Lisa Whedbee.

CHAPTER 34

The reporters said it was "a sexy story": church, greed, adultery, blood, a defenseless child with Down syndrome, all the elements that garnered column inches and high ratings, spurring readership and attracting viewers.

It didn't take long for the phones to start ringing once the morning paper hit the box. The attempt on Rob's life was front-page news. Most of Knoxville was in shock—an award-winning journalist and a stay-at-home mom conspiring to kill her husband. Crimes like that didn't happen in Knoxville. And as soon as the news hit the Associated Press wire, the whole country was reading about the "Tennessee Love Triangle." Reporters and producers from around the country, including *CNN*, the *Los Angeles Times*, the *Chicago Tribune*, the *New York Times*, and *People*, began showing up on Knoxville's doorstep, anxious to talk with anyone even remotely associated with the story. Even with all the fallout from the O. J. Simpson murder trial, the media's curiosity could not be quelled.

Michael Frazier and Lisa Whedbee were both in jail under a $50,000 bond, and Rob immediately began taking action to protect his family. Rob filed for divorce and sole custody of the children and took out restraining orders against Lisa and Michael Frazier. He also called about having a comprehensive security system put in his house. His hardest task would be telling his little boy his mother would not be coming home and arranging care for the children, so he could return to work. His parents, also in shock, immediately pitched in to help as much as they could.

Lisa was released on a $50,000 bond later that same day and was immediately placed under psychiatric care at Park West Hospital. Michael's parents made bond the following day, and Frazier was released and whisked away in his high-profile attorney's car. A preliminary hearing for the co-conspirators was set for July 7.

Rob was so busy that the actuality of what had happened had not really set in, but it would eventually catch up with him. For the time being, he was possessed by an all-consuming anger about his betrayal and for the people who planned his demise. Still, he didn't have time to let this terrible thing that had happened to him knock him down. He knew he must keep on going. Rob's focus had to be running his business and caring for his two, suddenly motherless, children.

Rob met with the prosecution team slated to handle the case against Frazier and Lisa and was advised to keep his mouth shut and not speak with the media. Even when the media began to claim Rob abused his wife and children, he had to remain silent—a bitter pill for Rob who never raised a hand against any member of his family, including his wife. Rob was embarrassed and worried how headlines like "Accused wife claims hubby abused her" and "Husband abusive, says wife charged in plot" would impact his business. Fortunately, Rob's clients were loyal and did not buy the tales told in the tabloids. Later, Rob vowed if he could do things differently, he would have most definitely spoken with the press to tell his side of the story—the truth.

CHAPTER 35

It was another sleepless night as Rob lay in bed analyzing the pieces of the puzzle that had now become evident to him. He believed from the very start, Lisa was playing him, trying to follow her mother's advice to marry a rich man; from "I get the driver" to the "suicide" attempt, straight through to the supposed pregnancy, Lisa had been manipulating him.

Rob began to think about his marriage of twelve years, and in retrospect, he clearly saw Lisa's erratic pattern of behavior—the weekends and late-night outings, her interest in his life insurance policy, the 911 calls, the attorney incident, her ongoing rejection of Brittany, and rumors of an affair. He should have realized something was going on, especially when recalling the incident where she met him with his loaded shotgun. Rob shook his head, which was pounding painfully in his ears. He went to the medicine cabinet to get something for his headache. When Rob opened the cabinet, he immediately noticed something strange. Prior to Britt's surgery for Moyamoya, she was prescribed liquid Valium to calm her and ease the pain. Rob was sure the bottle had been full the week before, but now, it was practically empty. Rob's blood turned cold. Had she also tried to murder Brittany?

One thing was blatantly clear: once Lisa had upped the ante from divorce to murder, her trail of premeditation could be easily tracked.

CHAPTER 36

Joyce and Lloyd Whedbee were founding members of Trinity United Methodist Church. It was the church where Rob was baptized and attended Sunday school as a boy. After Rob and Lisa married, Trinity became their church.

This also was where Lisa turned for solace after Brittany's birth, joining the choir, playing hand bells, and participating in many of the church's activities. Rob and Lisa had developed friendships with several other couples from the church, and on occasion, they would invite them to spend a weekend with them at their condo in Gatlinburg.

In addition to being where the affair between Lisa and Michael Frazier began, it was also where Rob and Lisa sought counseling when the foundation of their marriage began to crumble.

When tragedy strikes, a member of the church family there is the supportive outreach, but Rob was not prepared for the advice he would receive from Pastors Larry and Brenda Carroll.

When the Carrolls heard the news about the attempt on Rob's life, they did not seek him out, but, instead, immediately rushed to the jail. Sin or not, Lisa Whedbee and Michael Frazier were still important members who had given much to the church. The Carrolls felt that Michael and Lisa needed their support, and they felt it was their duty to provide it.

After Brenda and Larry returned from their visit at the Knox County jail, Larry immediately called Rob.

"How are you are doing, Rob, and how are the kids?" Larry asked.

"It's been difficult for me, but my main concern right now is protecting the children and maintaining a safe and stable life for them."

"I can understand that. Have you been to see Lisa?" Larry asked.

"No, Larry, and I don't intend to."

Larry went on to explain to Rob that he and Brenda had spent some time with Lisa that morning.

"I swear, Rob, she is so remorseful about what happened. She even admitted you never hurt her or the kids. She said you were a good person, and she is so sorry."

"I don't buy it, Larry. Lisa is sorry she got caught, and that's the only thing she is sorry about—, except maybe that she failed to kill me."

"Don't talk like that, Rob. Brenda and I both think you should give her another chance. You know the importance of forgiveness."

"Larry, are you really serious?" Disgust and disbelief were clear in his voice. "She tried to kill me, Larry—. KILL ME! You don't take somebody back after that."

"We just feel strongly that Lisa is sincere. She wants you back. She wants to fix your marriage. You should at least bail her out so the two of you can talk."

"Bail her out?" Rob was taken aback, and said once again, "She tried to kill me, Larry! "I'm not taking her back, I'm not forgiving her, and I'm damn sure not bailing her out."

The end of that conversation was the end of Rob's relationship with both the Carrolls and with Trinity United Methodist. Everyone seemed to be worried about Lisa and have little concern for Rob and the children. They had all lined up in Lisa's corner, and Rob had no use for them. Lloyd and Joyce, despite their longtime relationship with TUMC and many of its members, were hurt deeply by the response from the church. For them, the break was devastating.

Claiming to be in an ethical bind, neither Larry nor Brenda would ever admit to investigators or to the prosecution team that Lisa had confessed to Rob's innocence, claiming it was privileged information. Larry and Brenda Carroll had a distorted perception of "Christian charity," and Rob and his kids would get along just fine without them.

CHAPTER 37

His brain was once again hammering in his head when Rob opened his eyes. The red digital numbers on the clock beside the bed flashed seven fifty-four; Saturday morning was beginning. The Bayer aspirin in the medicine cabinet was calling, and Rob needed two of those and some coffee. He wanted to lay there a bit longer. His mind and body begged him to. It had been a long time since Rob Whedbee had gotten a good night's sleep. The memories of the attack that almost ended his life replayed in his mind. No matter how many weeks rolled by, the thoughts were always there.

He needed to check on Justin, so he threw on his robe, grabbed the bottle of Bayer, and strode to the kitchen to crank up the coffee maker. The kitchen overlooked the den, and there was Justin, sitting in front of the TV watching *Power Rangers*.

"Hey, Big Cat. Want some eggs?"

Without turning from the TV, he answered, "Froot Loops, Dad."

"Froot Loops it is."

Rob watched his blond-haired boy for a moment, wondering how he was doing. He'd been especially quiet since the attack, and he no longer liked playing in the front yard. Justin would run in the house anytime a strange car passed by. Rob had tried to explain to the nine-year-old what his mother had done. Justin never asked about his mom, and he almost seemed to dread the supervised phone calls Lisa made to her son every Thursday night. Rob worried about what was going on in that little head.

Rob poured some coffee and got the milk and eggs out of the refrigerator. Brittany would be awake soon, and she liked eggs and sausage. He sipped his coffee and got the cereal out of the pantry for his son.

Justin called from the den, "Dad, I hear Britt."

A small voice drifted down the hall, "Da-Da."

"That would be her," Rob said. "Justin, come get your cereal and then get dressed. We've got to go to the grocery store today."

"Can't I stay with Joyce and Pops?" Justin asked.

Rob's parents did usually keep the kids when he went to the store or had to run errands. Their support was immense, and life would have been a lot more challenging for Rob if they had not been there to help him navigate this major life change.

"Sorry, buddy, they're in Gatlinburg today, but you'll see them tomorrow."

Rob took another sip of his coffee before heading to Brittany's room. It would be long cold before he got back to it.

Britt lay in her crib staring up at Rob as he leaned over and smiled at her. She was the prettiest little girl with silky blond hair and an ivory complexion. In addition to being a Down's baby and suffering from Moyamoya disease, several stroke-like episodes had left her paralyzed except for her left arm, head, and neck. It broke Rob's heart to know she would never run or play. He'd never walk her down the aisle, but he loved that little girl and was fiercely protective of her. Lisa had wanted no part of Brittany and had begged Rob to put her in some type of facility. That ongoing argument contributed to the erosion of their marriage. He couldn't understand why Lisa couldn't see beyond Brittany's diagnosis. There was so much more to this precious child. Brittany may not have a "normal" life, but she was happy and had developed a personality. She was, for the most part, nonverbal, but she could most definitely express her moods and her likes and dislikes.

"Hey, Miss Britt," Rob said, smiling at her as he bent to pick her up.

He noticed the diaper had leaked, and he would need to strip the bed and put on fresh sheets, but first he cleaned her up and got her diapered. He pulled out her purple shorts and her Barney T-shirt and then carefully dressed her. All the while, Britt said Da-Da and made sounds no one understood. Da-Da would soon change to daddy, as Brittany learned a few words in the coming years, but the three she used most were "daddy," "yup," and "no." "Mommy" never became a part of her limited vocabulary.

Going to the grocery store with both kids was always quite a feat. It was a process just getting Britt in and out of the Suburban. Justin, very attentive to Britt, would be beside her in the back to keep an eye on her. Once in the store, Rob juggled pushing Brittany's wheelchair and the shopping cart as the three of them swung through the aisles, loading up the cart along the way. Rob tried not to block the aisle with his little entourage as they went up and searching through the shelves of food. People he passed would look at them, smile, and nod. Others would quickly avert their eyes as not to stare at the little girl with severe disabilities.

Once back home, Rob unloaded Britt, took her into the den, and put her in her special lift chair in front of the TV. He and Justin unloaded the grocery bags from the back of his truck. Afterward, Rob made lunch for the kids and sat down for a few minutes while he fed Brittany. Rob went through the house picking up dirty clothes and Britt's soiled sheets and started a load of laundry. He then asked Justin to watch her for about twenty minutes while he cut the front yard.

The day was a busy one, but they all were. Before dinner, Rob sat and played with Brittany for a while. Justin was downstairs in his playroom, constructing buildings out of Legos. For dinner, Rob grilled some boneless chicken thighs, steamed some broccoli, and made a salad. Justin ate in front of the TV while Rob fed Britt. Rob always ate after she was situated. Once done, he washed the dishes, folded clothes, and made up Brittany's bed. By eight thirty, Britt had her medications, had been changed, and was tucked snugly in her bed. Rob and Justin watched a motocross race, something Justin loved and would later enjoy competitively in his teenage years.

Around ten o'clock, Rob helped Justin get ready for bed, making sure he brushed his teeth and put his clothes away. Since the attempt on Rob's life, Justin refused to sleep in the dark, and Rob switched on the night-light that cast a soft glow across the room.

With both kids down for the night, Rob went back to the motocross race and began to flip through the *Knoxville News Sentinel*. Once again, the case was in the paper, and Rob cringed as he again read how Lisa alleged that he was abusive. It was an embarrassment to Rob who had never raised a hand to Lisa. The other line that bothered him was, "Whedbee only sustained minor cuts...." Sure, his ear had healed well, and the lacerations to his throat were gone. The cut to his thumb had severed the radial artery, but it too had healed. The articles seemed to imply because he had not been killed or seriously injured, the crime was not really that bad. The media never talked about the psychological injuries that would take much longer to heal, if they ever did.

Although Rob did what he had to do every day, he was consumed by anger and a pain that cut clean through his soul. He worried about the long-term impact this would have on Justin, and he wasn't sure he, himself, would ever be able to trust again. Despite everything, Rob was moving forward as best he knew how, working hard on the business and taking good care of his kids. There were no more softball games after work, no long afternoons of fishing, and no female companionship, but Rob accepted all of that, knowing his children needed him more than ever. He dearly loved his children and gladly gave them the time and love they needed, trying his best to make up for the mother they had lost. Rob pushed on, refusing to act like the victim, which, in fact, he was.

CHAPTER 38

Like boxers in a prize fight, the prosecution and defense squared off in the legal ring for *Tennessee v. Michael Frazier* trial. In the defense's corner stood a fair-haired, hotshot, young attorney named Greg Isaacs. Known to many as "Sweet Cheeks," Isaacs was a good-looking, charismatic individual who was just beginning to make a name for himself in Knoxville legal circles.

Bill Crabtree, deputy district attorney, headed up the prosecution. Crabtree, appropriately nicknamed "Crabby," was known as a bulldog who relied on time-proven, "old-school" prosecution to get the job done. If a case made the news, Bill Crabtree was called upon to handle it. A prosecutor since 1976, Crabtree had started his law career as a criminal defense attorney. Jo Helm, a highly respected member of the DA's office, made up the other half of the prosecution's team.

Officiating was the Honorable Judge Richard Baumgartner. A criminal court judge since 1992, Baumgartner had presided over seventy trials. Prior to serving on the bench, Judge Baumgartner was in private practice in civil law from 1972 until 1992. Baumgartner was known to be a smart and fair judge who wasn't afraid to speak his mind to maintain order in his courtroom.

The sparring began long before the trial with umpteen motions submitted by the defense. Legal bantering was exchanged on the front page of the *Knoxville News Sentinel*. During the fifteen months since the crime, the media's interest in the scandalous case had not subsided. The case had already been tried in the court of public opinion, and headlines screamed from the paper boxes.

Greg Isaacs had announced that he would use the affirmative defense of renunciation, claiming Frazier had changed his mind before killing Rob Whedbee. The prosecution had dropped the conspiracy charge against Frazier and were focused on the attempted first-degree murder charge. And with all the media hungry for anything to report about the case, a circus-like atmosphere surrounded the impending trial.

CHAPTER 39

Homicide was quiet on Tuesday morning. Dan Stewart kicked back and propped his feet up on the desk as he read the morning paper.

"God Almighty," he swore, throwing the paper across the room.

His partner, Larry Johnson, poked his head through the door to investigate the commotion.

"What's the problem, Dan?"

Dan reached for the paper and folded it to reveal a story.

"Have you freaking seen this?"

The headline read, "One charge on defendant in love triangle dropped."

"You've got to be kidding me."

Larry's deep baritone voice echoed around the room.

"They dropped the damn conspiracy charge," Dan said.

"What the…"

"Yeah," Dan said in exasperation. "Jo Helm said they needed to tidy up the case."

"Tidy up the case?" Larry asked. "We busted our asses getting them all the evidence they needed to make the conspiracy charge stick. What about the fake 911 call, the fact she brought him into her home, the evidence we found at their little love nest?"

Larry's voice boomed throughout the office as his rage grew. He was one of the most well-liked officers on the force, laid-back, and funny, with a voracious appetite for life. Just don't make him angry. As a litany of profanity poured from his mouth, officers were beginning to poke their heads out of offices and cubicles, wondering what had pissed off Larry Johnson.

Michael Frazier had been indicted by the grand jury on two counts: attempted first-degree murder and conspiracy to commit first-degree murder. The grand jury obviously thought there was enough evidence to indict him on both charges.

"The next damn thing they'll be saying is it wasn't premeditated," Dan said.

"God, they better not! We've got so much evidence. Howdy Doody could try this case."

"I've got a bad feeling about this case. I guess we'll just have to wait and see. Tidying up, my ass!" Dan exclaimed.

Dan had seen it before. So had Larry and most of the investigators on the force. You spend months investigating a case, crossing t's and dotting i's, putting together a clean line of evidence, and when it gets to the prosecution, they simply ignore some of the facts. It was highly frustrating for an investigator to spend that much time building a case, motivated by finding justice for the victim, and putting away the perpetrator. Dan felt sorry for Rob Whedbee. Two people had acted in concert to orchestrate his death, and the prosecution didn't have the fortitude to take it all the way.

CHAPTER 40

It was a hectic Monday morning at Whedbee Insurance, and the phones rang incessantly. Rob was covered up, handling claims from the weekends and trying to write several new policies, when Joyce called from the front office.

"Rob, Gerald Houser for you on line two."

Gerald was the condominium manager at Raven Crest in Gatlinburg where Rob owned the condo. Since the murder attempt and Lisa's release from the psych ward, she had been living there, awaiting her trial for attempted first-degree murder and conspiracy to commit first-degree murder.

Wondering what was up at Raven Crest, Rob picked up the phone.

"Gerald, how are you doing, and what can I do for you?"

"Hey, Rob...doing well. Getting ready for the ski season," he stated cordially. Then his tone changed and he said, "Rob, I hate to bother you with this, knowing all you've been through, but your neighbor below you is complaining about someone tossing cigarette butts from your balcony onto his property. I know that wife of yours is living up there, and I wondered if you could talk to her about it?"

"Cigarette butts?" Rob asked. "Lisa doesn't smoke." Just then the light bulb went on in his head, *Frazier*! Frazier was a chain-smoker. "Gerald, have you seen anyone up there with my wife, specifically a male?"

He told Rob he had seen Lisa coming and going on occasion, but she had always been alone.

"Gerald, I think my wife may be seeing Michael Frazier again, and if he's up there with her, she's going to find herself looking for a new place to live. I'd really appreciate it if you'd keep an eye on the comings and goings at my place. I'd bet money my would-be murderers are conspiring again."

"Sure, Rob. I'll let you know if I see anything suspicious."

As Rob hung up the phone, he could feel the fury building up inside him again. The court had forbidden Lisa and Michael from seeing each other after their release on bond. Yet Michael Frazier was enjoying the benefits of a place Rob was paying for. He'd be damned if he was going to let them get away with that. He immediately called his divorce attorney, Nelwyn Rhodes.

Nelwyn agreed Rob should not have to pay the expenses if, indeed, Lisa and Frazier were nesting in the Raven Crest Condo. Nelwyn also recommended Rob hire a private investigator to confirm that the two were still seeing each other and if he was staying with Lisa at the condo. The attorney gave Rob the name of an investigator she had used, and before long, Brian Norris, a self-employed PI, was on the case.

Norris, a friendly guy but a tenacious investigator, rented a condo at Raven Crest and set up surveillance of the activity at 413. On November 5 at 7:07 a.m., a man exited Rob's condo, got in the back seat of Lisa's Jimmy, and laid down. The PI had seen it all and couldn't help but laugh as he watched the man hide under a blanket in the back seat. About ten minutes later, Lisa came out of the condo and got into the driver's side of her SUV. Brian followed them into Gatlinburg where he observed the male subject sitting up and crawling into the front seat. Sure enough, it was Michael Frazier. Lisa and Frazier drove to a Walmart in Sevierville where Lisa parked next to Michael's Honda Accord. The two sat together several minutes, embracing frequently, which Brian was able to capture on video camera.

On Thanksgiving Day, Brian set out to follow Lisa's movements. As she raced to Kingsport at speeds in excess of 100 mph for most of the entire ninety-mile trip, Brian feared for his life but managed to stay with her without being noticed. Michael was waiting for Lisa at

Warrior's Path State Park where they had a romantic Thanksgiving Day picnic. Norris also shot video of their encounter.

When the news was released about the video evidence of the lovers' trysts, Greg Isaacs, Frazier's attorney, said, "It is, in the words of Shakespeare, 'much ado about nothing.' Whomever my client chooses to associate with should not be newsworthy."

"Much ado about nothing?" This evidence made a compelling case for the conspiracy charges against Lisa and Frazier.

CHAPTER 41

There was nothing small about Mickey Childress. She was bigger than life. A well-regarded investigator for the state attorney general's office, Mickey was a force to be reckoned with.

Born on a farm in Virginia just across the Tennessee border, Mickey came to Knoxville to play basketball at UT, racking up scoring records during her tenure. Voted into the Women's Basketball Hall of Fame, Mickey had traveled the country, playing on the All-American Red Heads, the first women's professional basketball team.

Joining the attorney general's office in the early eighties under Ed Dossett's administration, Mickey was well-regarded and highly respected for her fiery drive and hard work. Her ability to get people to open up was just one of the many facets that made her so good at her job.

Mickey passionately defended the innocent and sought to make sure the guilty were punished. She excavated layers of information, oftentimes with much difficulty, to support the district attorney's cases.

Assigned to the Michael Frazier case, Mickey wasted no time in contacting Rob Whedbee. In her no-nonsense way, she informed Rob she would be digging deep into his life as well as the lives of his estranged wife and her lover.

"If you have any skeletons in your closet," she told him, "this is your chance to shake them out because I will find them."

Feeling like he had finally found an ally, Rob liked her immediately and said, "Investigate away! I have nothing to hide."

Never one to mince words, Mickey went on to ask Rob, point-blank, if he was guilty of any of the accusations Lisa had made.

"I have not always done things perfectly. I've not always been 'Johnny-on-the-spot' with flowers and gifts at the right moment but," Rob continued, "I can assure you I never abused Lisa or did anything to deserve being murdered."

Mickey watched Rob as he spoke, nodding her head.

"Good," she said. "That's what I wanted to hear. Now," she said, laughing, "let's go get us some bad guys!"

Mickey conducted extensive interviews with more than thirty people associated with Rob and Lisa, both as a couple and as individuals. She went back as far as the teachers and coaches of both Rob and Lisa. Mickey accumulated overwhelming evidence that refuted Lisa's claims of abuse by Rob and revealed Lisa was not well-liked by some people. Her investigation left her with the impression that Lisa tended to be dishonest, and many interviewees felt she could not be trusted. Some talked about the many stories Lisa had told about her abuse as a young girl, having found them to border on the ridiculous. According to witnesses, Lisa had done drugs in high school and had once run away from home with a friend, hitching a ride with a trucker. Mickey felt, based on the discovery of her investigation, chances were strong that Lisa was the one lying, not Rob.

Mickey's investigation was thorough and revealed some surprising information that had not been heard before. She learned about Lisa's brief tryst with a Knoxville cop she had met at Tammy's pool and gathered details about Lisa's flirtatious nature. She had been told by a member of Trinity United Methodist that Lisa had come on to a male member at a party and was seen kissing him outside the church.

True to her word, Mickey took a hard look into Rob's life. Time and time again, she was told that Rob was an honest person and a good friend who could be trusted. She also heard that Rob had a weakness for contact sports, fast cars, motorcycles, and cheeseburgers.

She told Rob that several friends had said if they were serious about killing Rob, they would not use a knife.

Mickey Childress investigated the case for close to a year, giving the prosecutors plenty of damaging evidence. Unfortunately, she could not control what they would or would not use during the trial; and sadly, much of it would never be heard in court.

CHAPTER 42

Driving to the courthouse, Rob felt as if he was on his way to a boxing match. He felt the adrenaline pumping through his body like he was headed into the ring instead of Courtroom IV at the Knox County Courthouse. Getting ready that morning, it felt as if he should be gloving up rather than putting on a suit and tie.

It was now September, more than a year since the attempt on his life, and after three postponements, his day in the ring had finally arrived. He hoped he had the perseverance and mental fortitude for the bout he was facing.

Although he was the victim, it seemed as though the media had done a pretty good job of portraying him as the villain during the fifteen months that had passed. For all the time spent with his prosecution team, Bill Crabtree and Jo Helm, he felt ill-prepared for what was to come, and he knew the ring was a lonely place for an unprepared boxer.

Criminal Courtroom IV was designed with lightwood paneling and wooden pews that were filled to maximum capacity as relatives and spectators were anxious to finally see the much-hyped trial. A low hum of whispers and the swishing of people squeezing by others, in search of a perch, filled the room. Bailiffs, like hall monitors, circled the room, looking for anyone in violation of court rules. And there was a new presence in the courtroom. For the first time in Tennessee legal history, cameras were allowed in the courtroom, and Court TV, cable's legal channel, was there to provide gavel-to-gavel coverage of the *Tennessee v. Frazier* trial. Lisa Whedbee was noticeably absent at the trial of her "soul mate," as she would call him years later.

Outside the courtroom, a clamor of reporters, cameramen, and photographers, jockeying for position, could be heard, signaling the approach of Michael Frazier and his defense team of Greg Isaacs and Ron Rayson.

Isaacs, sharply dressed, radiated confidence and told the media before entering the courtroom, "Michael Frazier did not attempt to kill Robert Whedbee."

Every head in the courtroom turned as they entered. So here was the funny-looking man whose alleged actions had garnered so much media time and space.

At 8:54 a.m., the prosecution team of Assistant Deputy Attorney Generals Bill Crabtree and Jo Helm made their way to the prosecution's table and began to unpack files and notes vital to the trial.

The bailiff escorted the jurors into the jury box. Seven men and five women comprised the group, three African Americans and nine Caucasians, with ages ranging from twenty-six to sixty-eight.

At precisely 9:00 a.m., when the courtroom was called to order with an "all rise," the Honorable Judge Richard Baumgartner entered with his ebony robe rustling as he made his way to his post and was seated. Criminal court was in session.

Opening arguments were given with the prosecution laying out how Michael Frazier, filled with lust and greed, had willfully attempted to murder a sleeping John Robert Whedbee, his lover's husband. Jo Helm also addressed the defense's plans to use the affirmative defense of renunciation saying, "Failure is not renunciation."

Isaacs, a born thespian, delivered a metaphoric story about a choir boy and preacher's kid seeing the light and knowing he could not kill the sleeping man. He also outlined that "Mike" Frazier's only reason for being in the Whedbees' house was in defense of poor, battered Lisa Whedbee, the woman he loved.

CHAPTER 43

It wasn't until almost 9:30 a.m. when John Robert Whedbee, the state's star witness, was finally called to the witness stand to begin testimony. Once again, Rob could not help but think of boxing as he took the three steps up into the witness box, just as he had taken those regulation three steps up into the boxing ring during his Golden Gloves days.

The prosecution's questions revolved around the facts of the early morning attack on Rob, and so prompted by Assistant Deputy District Attorney Bill Crabtree, Rob went through the events of that night from hell, relaying the facts that were burned into his brain. His sense of terror and disbelief, and now anger, were all there raging inside of him, but he spoke calmly about the matter of facts, just as he had done on countless interviews and discussions with investigators, attorneys, and friends. The story was always the same no matter how much Rob wished he could change it.

He demonstrated how he had awakened to see a dark figure wielding a knife above him, poised to strike a deadly blow. He held his clenched fist above his head to show what he had seen the second his eyes opened. Greg Isaacs would later describe Rob as the "angry man in the red shirt."

Rob watched as the state's evidence was introduced and displayed for the jurors—his bloody T-shirt, the blood-streaked sheets and pillowcases, the blanket from his bed also covered in his blood, and finally the knife and bat. Rob explained how he exited the house as the prosecution showed a floor plan diagram of the Belfast home.

The state wrapped up its direct examination of Rob by asking him to identify his assailant. Rob stood up and said sternly, "It's Michael Frazier, the man right there," pointing to a clean cut, but squirmy-looking Frazier. Michael stared at a legal pad on the table in front of him and did not make eye contact with Rob.

This concluded the prosecution's examination of Rob Whedbee, at which point the jury was removed from the courtroom so that the prosecution and defense could make their arguments for why or why not certain evidence or lines of questioning should be presented to the jury.

Bill Crabtree opened, "Your Honor, if counsel intended to go into any crimes, wrongs, bad acts, or anything of that nature, specifically any question concerning alleged domestic violence, that matter should be taken up out of the hearing of the jury."

Judge Baumgartner pushed his horn-rimmed glasses up from their perch halfway down his nose and said, "Why don't you just tell us exactly what it is you want to raise of that nature, Mr. Isaacs?"

Animated like a Saturday morning cartoon, Greg Isaacs began his spiel, trying to justify the introduction of testimony of domestic violence, arguing that the state had opened the door by discussing motive in their opening statement.

Isaacs went on to say, "We want to question Mr. Whedbee about an agreed order of protection," explaining the order of protection outlined specific instances of the alleged abuse against Lisa Whedbee.

The legal wrangling continued as Mr. Isaacs outlined numerous points of his intended defense of Michael Frazier.

Rob, still under oath, sat in the courtroom feeling somewhat nauseated by the slick talking and peacock walking of the defense attorney.

"So," Isaacs continued, "if we cannot go into domestic violence, we are going to be hamstrung from putting on our affirmative defense...as we are entitled to...I guess the burden is on the state is to say why it's not admissible."

The debate went on and on with Judge Baumgartner interjecting his comments and questions sporadically. Third-party defense, renunciation, state of mind, motive rebuttal—all phrases batted back and forth. It began to sound like droning to Rob; however, he could see the writing on the wall. The defense was going to use Lisa's lies against him in order to destroy his character during cross-examination.

When Judge Baumgartner finally reached his decision, he announced, "Our rules address specific types of evidence, in particular, character evidence…evidence of specific instances of conduct. If you are going to allow somebody to be cross-examined about that, the court is required to ensure a finding is reasonable and its probative value outweighs its prejudicial effect, and the only way you can do that is to listen to the testimony. I feel compelled to do that."

With that, he called Rob back to the stand; and once again, Rob remembered his days of boxing, entering the ring to face his opponent. This time, however, he was ungloved.

Tennessee Trial Statute 405 allows a type of character testimony that is an essential element of the charge, claim, or defense. In other words, by destroying Rob's character through a line of questioning based on Statute 405, Greg Isaacs was able to strengthen his defense of Frazier by implying his reason in being in the Whedbee house on June 8 was to defend Lisa, not to kill Rob Whedbee.

Rob was taking a flurry of low blows and had no way to defend himself. It was like he had his hands tied behind his back. He was cut off every time he tried to elaborate on allegations from the infamous order of protection, leaving him to only answer charges with statements like "Absolutely not," "That is totally false," and "No, sir, I did not."

Despite Rob's repeated denials of raping or abusing Lisa, Greg Isaacs had turned the tables, and it suddenly seemed that Rob himself was on trial. Rob was like a tiger in a cage, and Greg Isaacs was poking him with a big stick, trying to elicit rage.

Isaacs was adept at wording questions in a damning way.

"Now, to me, that sounds like you just described something that was fairly violent…and involved a loaded gun and sending your wife to the hospital with a broken arm, correct?"

The jury did not know Lisa had been the one holding the loaded shotgun pointed at Rob's head, and as far as the hospital, Lisa went to the ER the following day, and the doctor's report showed the arm was perfectly normal. Isaacs would not let Rob explain.

Bill Crabtree summed it up pretty well when he told the judge, "There has not been one bit of testimony that has come out through this cross-examination that has related to the defendant...not one reference to what this defendant had knowledge of. Furthermore, Your Honor, Mr. Isaacs wants to ask questions for the sole purpose of the questions."

After yet another of many bench conferences, Mr. Isaacs's cross-examination of Rob continued, this time focusing on the night of the attack. As had occurred during the earlier questioning by the defense attorney, the questions seemed to be inflammatory, giving the impression Rob was so much stronger than his assailant, that it was unlikely Michael Frazier could have caused Rob any injury.

Crabtree objected, and once again, the two attorneys approached the judge for yet another bench conference to discuss the relevance of Isaacs's cross-examination.

"If it is not connected," Baumgartner ruled, "I am going to tell the jury that the testimony not be considered by them. I will tell them to disregard it."

The question hung in the air like a storm cloud. How do you get someone to unhear something?

After that bench conference, Greg Isaacs continued with his loaded questions about the night of the attack, still poking his stick at the caged tiger.

"You were groggy, trying to leave the room, and you sprang out of the bed, and you grabbed what you thought was a perpetrator, a burglar, correct?"

"Absolutely not," Rob answered, trying to contain his disgust.

Without a pause, Isaacs continued, "And isn't it true when you grabbed this person from behind, he gave up?"

"No, sir," Rob insisted.

"Are you saying he didn't engage with you, correct?"

The anger was rising, and Rob struggled not to show it. Greg Isaacs was trying to make him angry and to discredit Rob.

"That is *absolutely* false." Rob fired back.

Isaacs walked back and forth in front of Rob, looking at the jury rather than Rob as he basically rewrote the truth of what happened the night Rob was almost killed.

"Isn't true that the wounds you received were wounds that you got when you grabbed the silhouette from behind and pushed him to the floor, correct?"

"That is completely false."

"Mr. Whedbee, isn't the simple fact of this case that as you lay there sleeping…that if an individual wanted to take your life with that knife, they could and there was nothing you could do to stop them?"

"Apparently, he couldn't for some reason."

Greg Isaacs pounced on Rob's answer, "Apparently, he did not for some reason. I have nothing further."

The cross-examination was over. It had been a grueling day for Rob, more than six hours on the stand, and it wasn't over yet. Rob's frustration strangled him. He had never beaten his wife, but he sure would have liked to have punched Greg Isaacs's right about then.

Bill Crabtree began his redirect to hopefully clarify for the jury the events Mr. Isaacs had so deftly distorted.

"On the fifteenth, when your wife had the shotgun, just tell the jury how that first came about."

Rob went back through the disagreement that began at the church when Lisa learned Rob had allowed Brittany to go swimming with her brother at his parents without asking her about it.

"She got very upset about that and caused a scene at the church."

Rob went on to explain how things had escalated once they both arrived home.

"I found her in the downstairs den with the shotgun in her hands. She leveled it at my face, and she said—"

Isaacs was quick to object, but Rob kept going, "Buddy, I am through with you."

Judge Baumgartner admonished Rob and advised the jury to disregard the last comment.

"So she leveled the gun at your face. Go on," Crabtree instructed Rob.

"And I took off. I fled the house."

Rob explained when he had returned home, he had examined the gun to find it loaded and chambered with the safety off.

"It was ready to go."

During the redirect, Crabtree led Rob back through the events up to and including the night he was almost killed, at one point even asking for Rob to come down from the witness stand and demonstrate how his hand had been cut during the struggle with Michael Frazier.

Greg Isaacs had one last question during his recross and asked Rob if the knife in evidence was the one that caused his injuries.

Rob, emotionally and physically drained, was finally excused from the stand and left the courtroom. Lisa and Frazier may have failed to kill him in his bed, but on the stand, his character had been assassinated.

After Rob left the courtroom, Judge Baumgartner advised the jury not to consider the evidence about Rob's alleged conduct for proving abuse but rather only consider it to establish Frazier's state of mind.

"The issue is," Baumgartner went on, "Mr. Frazier's state of mind, and you can consider it for the purposes of determining what, if any, effect these acts of conduct had on Mr. Frazier."

Not only had the jury been instructed to unhear testimony, they had also been told how to use the testimony that was given—two extremely unrealistic expectations for mere mortals. Even the gods in all their glory and omnipotence would have had a difficult time with that.

CHAPTER 44

The state rested its case on Wednesday after testimony from Bill Shinn, Rob's next-door neighbor who helped him on the night of the attack; Gerald Weller, the first officer on the scene; and Joe Minor, special agent forensic scientist with the Tennessee Bureau of Investigation. Minor's testimony centered around the DNA evidence that showed Rob Whedbee's blood on Michael Frazier's pants and *Phantom of the Opera* shirt.

"Very well, ladies and gentlemen, the state has concluded their case. This is now the opportunity for the defense to put on any proof they choose," Baumgartner announced.

The judge's remark seemed to emphasize the playing field was not level for the prosecution and defense. The prosecution could only enter testimony that was supported by evidence, while the defense had much more leeway in creating reasonable doubt.

The defense called Dr. Diana McCoy, one of the most damning witnesses to the prosecution's case. Dr. McCoy was a regular expert witness for the defense in personal injury and criminal cases. She possessed a PhD in clinical psychology with a specialization in forensic psychology. The defense's goals were to provide insight into the mental state of Michael Frazier and to paint Michael as a sympathetic person.

Diana McCoy was a petite woman with short, dark hair, plain features, and clear-rimmed glasses. She frequently sipped water from a Styrofoam cup. Throughout her testimony, she spoke directly to the jury.

McCoy presented a psychological profile of Michael Frazier and recounted information Frazier shared with her as part of more than thirty-one hours of examination. Thus, third-party hearsay, not usually allowed in a trial, was permitted as part of her testimony, opening the door for discussion of any alleged statements Lisa Whedbee made to Michael Frazier, and she had hearsay testimony in droves.

McCoy said, "Psychological testing suggested that Michael is a person who is introverted. He keeps to himself. He is not…very spontaneous. He…has pretty low self-esteem and has an image of himself as a kind of weak, ineffectual person."

"He is someone," she continued, "who would experience life as rather empty and meaningless. He distances himself from others… and is depressed…moody, nervous, and contends with feelings of inferiority."

Perhaps Michael's personality is exactly why he made the perfect pawn for Lisa Whedbee.

Isaacs then asked Dr. McCoy to discuss Frazier's life and social history and, with this Jo Helm, asked to approach the bench.

"I would like for Your Honor to caution the jury that this recitation of social history goes only to what he told her, not to the truth of the matter."

Once again, Baumgartner ruled to allow the testimony without a caution to the jury.

"I will tell them. I won't tell them now, but I will tell them at the end of the testimony."

Following that testimony, Greg Isaacs asked Dr. McCoy if she had any considerations relating to Michael's relationship with Lisa Whedbee.

"I did."

"And tell us how that relationship evolved."

Michael had recounted to Dr. McCoy however since he had met Lisa some six or seven years ago, he had instantly felt a kind of chemistry with her. He said she was often on his mind, and though he married twice during that time, he felt as if he had only settled, thinking Lisa would always be unattainable. Usually, she was the last thing he thought of at night. Michael was a lovesick puppy.

Then, in May of 1993, not long after the award-winning Mother's Day story about Lisa was published, she made her "declaration" of love for Michael. Michael would later testify it was the best day of his life.

The relationship eventually evolved into a sexual one, and the two would frequently discuss divorcing their spouses so they could be together. Lisa portrayed her husband as a bully and brute who tended to settle things with violence.

Frazier told McCoy about the apartment he had rented in March of '94, and in April, Lisa began to relay the stories of abuse and talking about wanting to kill her husband. She talked about dropping something heavy on his head, and then she progressed to saying she wanted to use a baseball bat.

Then McCoy began a litany of horrific things Michael told her Lisa allegedly told him: choking, rape, pornography, death threats, and violent beatings. If the abuse Lisa had suffered was so severe, why had no doctor or officer of the law ever seen anything? No one, except for Michael, Lisa's friends Tammy, and Debbie, and her mother had claimed to see the evidence of abuse. *Once again, why had no one thought to take pictures or call the police.*

Fact or fiction, Dr. McCoy continued to relay Michael's revelations to the jury. He talked about his growing concern for Lisa's well-being. At one point, he was convinced if Rob didn't kill Lisa, she would kill herself. Lisa began to talk about killing Rob almost every day.

Greg Isaacs asked Dr. McCoy to elaborate.

"He said that sometime earlier when Lisa was telling him 'I can't do it. I can't do it,' she asked him if he would do it, and he said yes. He would do it for her. He would kill Rob Whedbee for her."

At the end of Diana McCoy's testimony for the defense, the prosecution expressed concern to the judge that McCoy had given testimony that was not in any of the reports in their possession. The jury was dismissed for lunch so that Crabtree and Helm had time to review McCoy's file.

Following the return of the jury, Bill Crabtree cited a precedent that says, "Although a physician may give the defendant's history as related to him by the defendant, such history is not substantive evidence to establish truth." That was just one of the things the jury really didn't understand.

The first thing the prosecution set about in their cross-examination of Dr. McCoy was to establish that almost all information in which Dr. McCoy's findings were based on came directly from Michael Frazier.

Jo Helm opened by asking, "Most of the background data that you told the jury about the defendant, including the reported child abuse, revolves around the defendant telling you about that. Doesn't it?"

"Most of the data came from Mr. Frazier."

Jo Helm continued, "All the events recorded in the defendant's description of the incident related to Lisa Whedbee, which you testified about to the jury, were told to you by Michael Frazier, were they not?"

"Yes."

"You did not interview Lisa Whedbee at any time, did you?"

"I did not."

"You did not interview Rob Whedbee, did you?"

"I did not. All this information from Mr. Frazier was primarily what he had been told by Lisa Whedbee."

"And Mr. Frazier's first mental health care, psychiatric and psychological counseling, was when he came to you on June 22, 1994?"

"I'm sorry. He…actually, he went for marriage counseling I believe at his church several years ago."

"You think he did?" Jo Helm asked, expressing half-shock for the sake of the jury. "So his first interview was after the attempted first-degree murder charge?"

"Yes."

Jo probed more on the marital counseling, learning Dr. McCoy had not even requested records from that counseling.

Jo Helm then mounted another attack against the doctor's testimony, citing the Diagnostic and Statistical Manual of the American Psychiatric Association.

"Doctor, did you base your diagnosis of post-traumatic stress syndrome on this manual?"

"Yes."

"I would ask you if the last paragraph, which says, 'Malingering should be ruled out first in those situations in which…forensics determination play a role.'"

Malingering means fabricating or exaggerating the symptoms of a mental or physical disorder for a variety of secondary motives such as getting a lighter criminal sentence.

Greg Isaacs jumped to object, but Judge Baumgartner allowed the use of treatise to cross-examine.

"Thank you, Your Honor." And he said to McCoy, "You have read that, and you consider that part of what you are supposed to consider, do you not?"

"Certainly. Whenever I am interviewing anyone facing criminal charges, I consider the issue of malingering."

"But there is nothing whatsoever in this report that indicates whether you considered it, found it, or ruled it out, isn't that true?"

"It is never in any report, but it is always considered anytime an assessment is done."

"Okay," Helm said. "So it just didn't make it into the report?"

Getting somewhat indignant, McCoy answered, "It never makes it into any report unless I decide the person is malingering, and then that is one of the diagnoses."

The prosecution dug in for a big finish.

"Referring back to the DSM, there is a cautionary statement, is there not?"

"There is," McCoy answered.

"Okay. Would you look at the last sentence and tell me if you agree with me that it says, 'The clinical and scientific consideration involved in categorizing these conditions as mental disorders may not wholly be relevant to legal judgments.'"

"That is what it says."

"Dr. McCoy, were you paid for your work with Michael Frazier?"

"I was paid for the time I spent with Michael Frazier, yes."

"How much were you paid?"

"Uh, I'm paid 150 an hour and paid 250 per hour in court. I don't know the total at this point."

"Okay. So $150 for thirty-one and a half hours plus $250 an hour for the time you have been here today?"

"Yes."

"Dr. McCoy, it is a fair statement, is it not, that if the material on which you base your conclusions and diagnoses is false, then your diagnoses is wrong?

Dr. McCoy looked puzzled and said, "I'm not sure what you are asking me."

"If the information you have been provided from your various sources, including the defendant, is false, that would render your diagnosis faulty or invalid. Is that not true?"

"If everybody has given me false information, then obviously, it is false."

And having done their best to establish doubt about the "expert" testimony, the prosecution was done with Forensic Psychologist, Dr. Diana McCoy.

CHAPTER 45

Lying under oath is a crime, but it frequently happens in many trials—almost as an accepted element of any trial. A witness will stand before the court and swear to tell "the truth, the whole truth, and nothing but the truth," but inevitably, someone climbs into the witness box and spits out a lie or two.

Perjury typically occurs when a person makes a false statement under oath with the intent to deceive. In Tennessee, perjury is a Class A misdemeanor except under certain circumstances. Aggravated perjury, on the other hand, occurs when a person makes a false statement during or in connection with an official proceeding, and the false statement is "material" to the outcome of the trial. Aggravated perjury is classified as a class D felony and carries a two- to twelve-year sentence, if convicted.

According to Neil P. Cohen, University of Tennessee professor of law (retired), the charge of perjury is almost never pursued. Judge Roderic Duncan stated in his 1992 article, "Lying in Court," "There is rarely any earthly punishment for lying in court." There seems to be little deterrent to keep a witness from telling outrageous lies on the stand as happened with the defense's next three witnesses in *Tennessee v. Michael Frazier.*

Lisa's best friend, Tammy, was first on the stand and seemed to have no problem describing the dreadful bruises she had allegedly seen on Lisa.

"I initially saw the first bruise on her arm when her arm was in a brace. She was black from her wrist all the way to her elbow."

That was the arm Lisa went to St. Mary's ER about. However, medical records from that visit contradicted her statement. The ER doctor's findings were that Lisa's arm was normal. Did the trained medical staff miss the massive bruise? A bruise of that scope and nature would be almost impossible to hide and would take weeks to heal. Furthermore, there were no photographs to substantiate Tammy's claims.

Tammy went on to discuss other bruises she had allegedly seen. "On June 2, I saw bruises up her back, down the backs of her legs, and horrible purple black bruises between her legs."

Friends gathered around Rob's parents' pool about the same time in question, never saw the alleged bruises when Lisa was swimming.

Finally, Tammy's own statement to Mickey Childress conflicted with her trial testimony. During an interview with Mickey, Tammy stated, "Around Easter of this year, Lisa started telling me Rob was hitting her. She said one night, he pinned her to the floor, had his knee in under her chin, and the other knee between her legs. She showed me the bruises on her legs. I never saw bruises on Lisa other than that one time." Tammy went on to say, "I never told Rob that I knew the abuse was not true."

The second person to lie under oath was Lisa's mother.

Greg Isaacs asked about May 15, 1994, "Did you receive a call from your daughter?"

"Yes, I did."

"As a result of that call, what did you do?" Isaacs asked.

Jo told the jury that she went rushing over as quickly as she could. When she arrived, Lisa and Rob were standing in the front hall with two police officers.

"Did you observe any bruises, any wounds?" Isaacs asked.

"Yes, her arm, I thought, was broken. There was a big knot on it…and, uh, it looked to me like it had been bent. Also, she had many bruises on the inside of her upper legs. They were dark blue in color, and they looked a whole lot, to me, like fingerprints, and it wasn't just two or three. It was probably a dozen or more."

Jo said Lisa told her Rob had done it.

Gary Goins, one of the two Knox County officers at the Whedbees' home, had just finished examining Lisa and would later testify he had seen no evidence of abuse. How could an officer trained to spot signs of abuse miss the injuries Jo Outlaw described?

Finally, the last witness prior to the much-anticipated testimony of Michael David Frazier, was Lisa's close friend, Debbie. Debbie had some confusion about the actual date she had seen Lisa's bruising but claimed that on the fifteenth, Lisa had visited her, wearing a brace and sporting bruises on her left arm, while she had been in the hospital. Debbie described the alleged bruises as red and angry looking, and they were starting to change colors.

Although not brought out in court, Debbie would make an appointment for Lisa to see Dr. John Dagnon, the orthopedic surgeon for whom she worked. While sitting in the office waiting for the appointment, Lisa was observed by an employee of the doctor's office who stated in an interview with Mickey Childress that Lisa was not wearing a brace and that she saw no visible signs of bruising.

It seemed like there were a lot of lies flying around Courtroom IV, but even though the prosecution had access to all the information necessary to impeach all three witnesses, the suggestion of perjury never came up.

CHAPTER 46

Every occupant of Courtroom IV had been waiting for the appearance of Michael Frazier on the stand. They had seen him in the papers. They had seen him on TV. They had watched him sit without emotion for the three days of the trial, and now finally, they would hear him speak and see if he could answer charges that he had attempted the first-degree murder of Rob Whedbee.

Greg Isaacs had spent more than thirty hours preparing Michael for this moment. He was confident that his client was well-prepared. Michael walked to the stand with his head held up high with a sense of certainty. He was sworn in, and as he sat down, he immediately made eye contact with the jury—pure Greg Isaacs.

When Greg asked him to tell the jury a little about his background, he almost actually smiled before he began, again eyes sweeping the jury trying to show them he was just a poor misunderstood man, and they should care about him.

Michael congenially told the jury about his childhood in Kingsport, growing up the oldest son of a Baptist minister, living in the parsonage that was adjacent to the church. He had one younger brother named Terry, and throwing in a big smile, he said, "He and his wife just recently had a little baby girl named Michaela." It just seemed every word and every gesture was delivered with precision for the effect.

Michael went on to tell where he went to high school and college and to briefly discuss his employment background.

"After college, I immediately went to work at Trinity United Methodist Church in Knoxville as the organist. I was there until June of 1994, ten years. In 1988, I went to work for the *Oak Ridger* news-paper, first as an editorial assistant, and then through various promotions, I wound up as features editor."

His words were phrased nicely to show his hirability, promotability, and dependability.

Finally, after a chatty description of his various job duties at Trinity UMC and the *Oak Ridger*, Michael got to the name everyone had been anticipating as Isaacs asked, "What was your impression of Lisa?"

"Well, I was immediately drawn to Lisa. I had…I felt a very strong chemistry with her. And as I got to know her better, that intensified."

Just to keep it nice and honest, Greg told Michael to tell the jury a brief history of his marital background and got that out of the way.

"Now, at some point, your relationship with Lisa, I think you described it as a friendship, changed as you worked together at the church?"

To which Michael explained how, as he and Lisa worked together over a period of years, their friendship deepened, and then, of course, came the big Mother's Day story that was published in May of 1993.

"It was published on Mother's Day. It was a Mother's Day story. That's what it was designed to be. The Whedbees' daughter, Brittany, had been born with Down syndrome and with a heart problem, a defect, which required surgery at a very young age. Just a few months old, and Brittany was a real trooper, and she came through the surgery just fine. And then later, she began to have strokes and was just nearly dead. They took her to all kinds of doctors and had all kinds of tests to determine what was wrong with Brittany and what could be done about it."

Michael went on to tell about Brittany's medical issues and her brain surgeries, almost as if he was the concerned father.

"She had pretty much recovered from the surgeries but still had some problems from the strokes, but she was recovering. She was just a beautiful little girl, and I thought it would make a dramatic and heartwarming story for Mother's Day. So I decided to write it."

Michael continued with his "touching" story about the article "A Mother's Nightmare: A Mother's Dream" and how it went on to win a statewide journalism award.

"Lisa was very excited about it."

Of course, she was. In the article, she was cast in the role of a saint—a far cry from the woman who had asked "How do we get out of this?" when Brittany was born.

"Lisa received a lot of attention, cards, comments, and notes from organizations, support groups, and things like that, and she was very excited about the article."

"Tell the jury how your relationship changed, if it did, after that point," Isaacs directed.

Michael's story continued to unfold as he recounted the details of the night after choir practice when Lisa had "declared" her love to him.

"Well, I couldn't believe it. It…uh…I was just floored by the fact that after I had felt the way I had for so long. And she came to me and said she felt the same way…I just couldn't believe it. It was like the best thing that had ever happened, and, uh, I was overwhelmed."

The next day, Lisa went to the beach with her family for two weeks, but as she had promised Michael, she called him several times.

"We talked for just a few minutes on those occasions. It was just sort of silly, childish high school kind of conversation, giggling and not wanting to hang up, but not really knowing what to say."

The day Lisa returned from the beach, she met Michael in a restaurant parking lot, and they talked about that Wednesday night after choir practice when they both had admitted their feelings for each other.

"We sort of reaffirmed that we did have these strong feelings for each other and that they had been there for a long time."

"Did your relationship become physical?" Isaacs asked.

"No, it did not, not at that point. We went on a short trip to Chattanooga a few days later. We had never really had a chance to talk one-on-one except for the interview, except for, you know, just a few minutes at a time. We'd never really had an in-depth conversation about ourselves. We really wanted to get to know each other better. And so we went on a long drive one day and ended up in Chattanooga, and then we drove back. And, uh, that was the day Lisa and I first held hands, and we first kissed. It took on a completely different tone after that kiss. There was no way it was just an innocent little flirtation anymore because we shared a kiss, and we shared a secret."

Isaacs asked, "Did you have strong feelings for her?"

"Very strong."

Michael explained of their growing relationship.

"We talked every day on the phone. We, uh, became closer. We tried to see each other for a few minutes whenever we could. And we did. The relationship did become sexual at the end of July."

"Now," Isaacs asked, "was the main part of this relationship physical? Was this a lusty, sexual affair you and Lisa were having?"

"No, sir, it was not."

"How often would you have sexual relations?"

"Well, not more than once a month throughout the whole relationship, and it was a long time after we professed our feelings, our love for each other, before we ever did."

One Court TV commentator would say it sounded like Michael was describing a sweet courtship between two star-crossed lovers rather than a union that would end in conspiracy to commit first-degree murder.

Isaacs then moved toward Michael's awareness of the condition of Lisa's marriage. Michael acknowledged that he became aware from what Lisa told him that she was an abused wife and that Rob was a bully.

Lisa told me, "He mistreated her, pushed her around, and he had even raped her."

"And how did this make you feel, Michael?"

"It made me angry. This was someone I loved, and someone I considered very valuable. To think that she was being treated that way, I was...uh...I was disgusted by it, and I was angry."

With a pained expression on his face, Michael, the award-winning storyteller, told the jury about how the (alleged) abuse escalated.

"In the spring of 1994, the abuse was intensifying. I was seeing more bruises. I would see bruises on her arms that had the shape of fingerprints as if her arm had been squeezed. And there were sometimes bruises on her neck...uh...the bruises on her thighs."

He talked about how Lisa was wasting away. He said, "She was losing weight dramatically fast, and she was shaking. She was trembling."

What was her emotional condition at this time?" Isaacs asked with a sympathetic tone.

Ah, actors on a stage and no one in the courtroom wanted to miss one moment of the drama. All necks were craned toward the witness box, and they hung on every word.

"Lisa was very upset, almost always crying. She was very depressed and very upset."

Michael described his own emotional state as very depressed, very hopeless, saying, "I wanted to help her, but I didn't know how to help her. And so I...I had a very hopeless, depressed feeling as I watched her just waste away."

Moving ahead, Greg Isaacs said, "Let me direct your attention to the last week of May and the first week of June of 1994." He asked, "Did Lisa relate to you that the situation was changing with her husband, Rob?"

"Yes, she did."

"Tell the jury what she told you and what you observed."

Michael sighed deeply and said, "On first day of June 1994, I...uh...I got a phone call from Lisa. She was frantic. She was very upset...told me she needed to see me right away. And so I went to see her. We met at the lake. And when I got there, I got into her car, and she was crying uncontrollably. And she couldn't talk, and I didn't know what was wrong."

Lisa eventually got herself together enough to tell Michael what had really been going on in her life for the previous months.

"Her tone was, uh, very confessional. It was...I mean, it was very sad and very hopeless, and she told me that Rob was repeatedly raping her. He said she didn't deserve to live that...uh..."

Michael took a long pause as if to collect himself. "That nobody would want her, and she was just very upset, and I was very upset."

"The next day, Lisa called me, and her voice sounded funny. I knew something was wrong, and she started telling me that she was sorry that she had ruined my life and that she knew that nobody could ever love her again. She was going away and leave everybody alone, and I assumed that she was going to commit suicide. And I told her, 'Don't. Don't do anything until I get there. And if it has really come to that, then we'll do it together.'"

Of course, suicide had worked for Lisa in the past, and it seemed it worked for her this time too as Michael dropped everything and rushed to her home.

"Tell the jury what you saw when you arrived at Lisa Whedbees' home," Greg asked.

"I ran in through the front door, and I…I heard something down the hall to my right. Lisa was in the bathroom…just kind of draped over the toilet, just throwing up into the toilet. And, uh, she had taken a great deal of medicine…eight of whatever it was."

Did it cross any one of the jurors' minds that eight of almost anything is unlikely to kill someone, and surely, an intellectual like Michael Frazier would have known that.

"When she was able to stop throwing up, I told her we had to walk. I didn't want her to go to sleep. She told me she thought all the medicine had come up, and I thought she seemed okay, but I didn't want her to go to sleep. And so we walked, and we walked, and we walked through the house. And I was still remembering all the things that she had told me about the day before, and she told me Rob raped her again the night before, that, uh, he choked her, and she said that she wanted to kill him while this was going on."

Isaacs prompted Frazier, "Did she think she was going to be killed by her husband?"

"Yes, sir. He had told her that repeatedly. He had demonstrated how he was going to do it, how he was going to snap her neck, and throw her down the steps, and tell everybody that Lisa had had a horrible accident."

"Did you believe her when she told you this?" the defense attorney asked.

"I did then, yes. I believed all of it."

"Tell the jury your mental state. How did you feel as you saw Lisa in this condition, and she related what her husband was doing?"

"I felt hopeless. I felt worthless. There was nothing I could do. This was the only person I had ever really loved. She was routinely beaten, raped, and humiliated, and there was nothing that I could do about it…and I felt suicidal."

Michael then began to talk about the events of June 7, and people in the courtroom leaned forward, and the courtroom filled with a silence like death. It was finally coming—Michael Frazier's account of what happened.

"What time did you leave work on the seventh of June?"

"Five o'clock, maybe, in the afternoon. I don't know…it was afternoon."

"What was going through your mind when you left work on that day, Mr. Frazier?"

"I don't remember what was on my mind. It was just a blur…I couldn't believe everything that was going on. I don't know what I felt. It was something indescribable. It was just indescribably bad. I was…I mean I knew I had to find some way to help this person that I loved so much but didn't know what to do…it was just hopeless, helpless rambling inside my head."

"You left work at five o'clock. What happened next?"

Perhaps Michael had forgotten his line as he paused for a long moment.

"Okay. On the way home from work…"

Michael paused again.

"I didn't know what might be coming up. I stopped, and I got a pair of rubber gloves…and I drove home."

"What happened next?"

"It was sometime after seven o'clock. Lisa came to my apartment and picked me up."

Michael Frazier told the courtroom that Lisa had been hysterical, crying, shaking, and suicidal again. She told Michael she was just sure Rob was going to kill her that night. Rob was going to kill her.

"Tell the jury what happened next."

"I got into the car, and I told her I would help her however I could, and so we drove to her house. I went into the house with Lisa, and she handed me a knife and told me to wait downstairs in a closet."

So Michael was waiting in a storage closet in the fetal position with a knife in his gloved hands, waiting for his one true love to tell him when she needed him. Michael would tell the court that he had kept his mind occupied by working crossword puzzles in his head and counting backwards from one thousand by seven.

Greg Isaacs asked, "Were you calm?"

"No, no," Michael began. "I was, uh, shaking. My heart was thudding. Physically, it was the most stressful feeling I have ever felt."

"What happened next?"

"At some point, Lisa opened the closet door, and, uh," another pause, "she told me to come out. She said, 'I need you,' and I said, 'Okay.' And she said, 'I'm scared,' and I said, 'I am too.'"

"How did she appear?"

"Lisa was scared. She was shaking. She was trembling, and her eyes were wide, and there were dark circles under them. Well...she looked hopeless."

Was he trying to describe a woman who had spent the evening leisurely painting her fingernails, putting on a sexy nightie, and seducing her husband?

"What did you do next?" Isaacs asked.

"I walked up the steps."

Michael told the courtroom that he went up the stairs very tentatively.

"I...uh...I didn't know what I was going to find when I got to the top of those stairs. I mean, I didn't know if there was a fight going on. I didn't know what had happened that she needed me."

"Did you have a knife in your hand?"

"Yes, I did."

"Tell the jury how you were carrying the knife."

"I had the knife in my right hand with the blade pointed down. It was by my side."

"Once you reached the top of the stairs, what did you do next?"

The courtroom was spellbound.

Michael continued, "Lisa said, 'He's in there,' and she pointed toward the end of the hall, so I turned toward the bedroom."

"Well, I walked down the hall, and into the bedroom, and then made my way around the foot of the bed. I turned the corner, and there was a window."

Michael said he was moving very slowly, waiting for his eyes to adjust. He could make out the shapes of furniture, but that was all.

"You were walking toward the bed, and you saw a window. Tell the jury what happened next."

"Well…there was light coming through the window."

"Are we talking about a lot of light?"

"No, it was just a dim light. It was the only light, but it was enough for me to see Rob lying in bed."

"Now, when you were walking around the bed, were you walking around, knife raised, ready to take his life?"

"No, no. I still had the knife in my hand down by my side."

"You were around the bed. Tell us what happened."

"Well, I saw him. I…uh…when I saw him…when the light let me see him, I realized that this was crazy, that there is no way I am going to kill anybody. There is no way I could kill anybody, and I certainly can't kill a man who is just lying there in his bed. And I looked at him, and I was able to…just make out his features enough to see that this wasn't the horrible monster that I had made him out to be. It was…it was just a man lying in his bed, and I couldn't kill him."

Isaacs had been waiting the whole trial to reveal the great metaphor he had developed as the crux of the defense. Preacher's kid saw the light and couldn't kill. He was savoring the moment as he asked, "What did you do next?"

"Well, I turned to…to leave the room…to get out of the room."

"What was going through your mind at this point, Mr. Frazier, as you turned?"

"Well, I was afraid. I mean I couldn't believe the position I was in. I was…I had never imagined myself, of all people, to be in a situation like that. I just couldn't imagine how it had happened. I knew that the only thing I had to do…the most important thing I had to do was to get out of that room right then, and that is what I wanted to do."

"So what did you do?"

"So I turned around, and I started out of the room. I started toward the door, and I ran into the bed."

"What did you do after you hit the bed?"

"I froze. When I hit the bed, it shook, and Rob stopped snoring, I just stood there, praying he would go back to sleep, or he would not wake up. And then he said, 'Lisa, what are you doing?' and I knew he thought I was Lisa, so I didn't say anything. Then he said it again, and I could hear him moving, and then I could feel his arm…his hand on my arm, pulling me back, and he asked me what I was doing. He still thought I was Lisa, and then he pulled me down to the floor, and he said, 'You're not Lisa.' And he started hollering for Lisa over and over as he held me there on the floor."

Michael explained even though the knife was still in his hand, he was not using it as a weapon and that he did not struggle with him.

"When he first grabbed me, I was off balance. Then, I flailed. I mean, I tried to maintain my balance, and that may have been when I cut him. But I didn't use the knife. I mean, I did not attack him with the knife. I tried not to hit him with the knife."

"What happened next?"

"Well, he was screaming for Lisa. He was telling Lisa, 'Come in here. There's somebody in the house.' I just sat there. You know, I gave up. He was hanging onto me. He had me in a bear hug with his arms around my arms. He was holding my hands down on the bed, and he kept calling for Lisa to come in and…to come in and help him. Then, at one point, he tried to call the police. He tried to reach the phone, and he grabbed both my hands in one of his while he was trying to use the phone. Then Lisa came in the room, and she had a baseball bat."

"What was your understanding as to what Lisa was going to do with that baseball bat? Rob told her to turn on the lights and call the police."

But Frazier explained she didn't do either thing.

"She came over to his side of the bed and, uh, told Rob, 'Just let him go. We just must get out of the house.'"

"What did Rob do?"

"He pushed her away, and she walked to the other side of the bed and put the bat down and told him again, 'We just have to get out of this house.' And that is when he threw me…under the night-stand, sort of, and then he ran out of the house."

"Did you pursue Robert Whedbee with a knife as he ran out of his home?"

"No, sir, I didn't."

"Tell the jury what you did after he threw you down."

"I stayed there for a while. I thought I had come very near to being killed, and my mind wasn't working. A few minutes later, Lisa came to me and helped me up and said, 'You have got to get out of here.' And I knew she was right. I knew I had to get out of that house, so I went down the hall to the kitchen door and looked out into the garage. Rob was standing at the garage door, beating on the gutter with the bat and yelling for his neighbor to come and help him. So I turned around and went back through the den and…out the sliding glass doors…"

"Mr. Frazier, when you went to 7500 Belfast Lane on Tuesday, June 7, did you, in your mind and your heart, believe Lisa Whedbee was in imminent danger from her husband?"

"Object to leading, Your Honor," Bill Crabtree said.

"What did you think?" Isaacs rephrased.

"I thought Lisa Whedbee was going to be killed."

"What was Rob Whedbee's condition when you entered that bedroom?"

"Rob was asleep."

Greg Isaacs was ready for a big finish and asked, "If you would have wanted to do bodily harm to Mr. Whedbee, was there anything that would have prevented you?"

"No, no. If I had wanted to kill him, I could have killed him."

"How do you feel about this?"

"Well, I feel terrible about it. I am…you know, I am horrified at what I allowed to happen to myself, that I couldn't think rationally, that I wasn't able to make sense of everything going on. I still can't believe it. It couldn't be me that even considered this. But I know that it was, and I am very sorry about everything that has happened."

"We have nothing further," Greg Isaacs said, grinning broadly as Michael Frazier was excused from the stand for a break before cross-examination.

His direct had gone close to perfect, and he was feeling damn pleased with himself and with Michael's performance.

CHAPTER 47

Michael Frazier's composure had gotten him through the direct by Greg Isaacs but evaporated quickly under the cross-examination of Bill Crabtree. He no longer looked at the jury congenially. In fact, he found little time to look at the jury at all.

Assistant District Attorney General William Crabtree had been waiting for this moment and voraciously sprung at Michael. He quickly established that Frazier was indeed having an affair with Lisa Whedbee and then jumped right to the heart of the matter.

"Also, sir, there is no question, is there, that in the early morning hours of June 8, 1994, you were in the bedroom of Rob Whedbee? Any question about that?"

"No, that is true."

"And there is no question, is there, sir, that at the time that you were in that bedroom, you were armed with a knife?"

"I was."

"And, also, sir, before going into that bedroom, you had been hiding in a closet in the Whedbee house for a period of, what, five, six hours?"

"I had been in a closet. I don't know how long."

Crabtree pointed out the math—if Lisa picked him up at seven o'clock and he came out of the closet around one in the morning.

"I don't know what time it was."

Crabtree brought up the knife again, trying to get Frazier to admit he planned to kill Rob with it; however, Michael responded at least eleven times that his sole purpose for being in the Whedbee home, holding a butcher knife, was to "protect Lisa."

"Sir, is it not true that you came out of that closet and went up those stairs for the sole purpose of killing Rob Whedbee?"

"No, sir."

"And in protecting Lisa Whedbee, you were going to take the life of Rob Whedbee?"

"I was going to do whatever I had to do to *protect Lisa.*"

"Well, what did you intend to do to protect Lisa?"

"I didn't know. I didn't know what the situation was going to be, and so I didn't know what I was going to have to do."

"Well, whatever you were going to do, you were going to do it with that knife, weren't you?"

"If I needed it."

"So that was the purpose of the knife, to do whatever you were going to do to Rob Whedbee. Is that correct?"

"Whatever I needed to do."

"What did you plan on doing with the knife?"

"I had planned on *protecting Lisa,* however I had to."

Michael's discomfort had become obvious to the jury and those in the courtroom.

Crabtree continued, "So you are sitting there in the closet with this knife to protect Lisa Whedbee. Was she going to come and tell you when she was in danger? Was that the plan?"

"There was no plan."

That was one of at least thirty lies Michael would tell on the stand during the cross-examination, proven by such documents as Diana McCoy's report and Lisa Whedbee's statement to Investigator Dan Stewart after she had waived her rights. Bill Crabtree never let up, wearing away at him until Frazier tripped up good. It was coming; Bill Crabtree was sure.

"There was no plan? You were just going to go sit in that closet, period?"

"I was going to be available. I was going to help her."

"And you were going to do it with the knife?"

"I had a knife. I was going to do it however I had to do it."

Michael explained he and Lisa had not discussed anything specific about what they were going to do and that he was there to help her because she thought she was going to be killed.

"That night?" Crabtree asked.

"That is why I went there, yes."

"That is why you went there that night. She was going to be killed that night over all other nights that all this had happened. You were there to protect her."

The DA went on to say, "When she came down to get you, she took you up the steps. Is that correct?"

"She went up the steps ahead of me."

"And the house was dark?"

"Yes, sir."

"You didn't see Rob Whedbee looming there with a shotgun or anything?"

"No, sir."

"But you've still got your knife. Did you ask her, 'What are we going to do?'"

"No, I didn't. She said, 'Michael, I need you.'"

Michael repeated his earlier testimony about both him and Lisa being afraid. Crabtree continued to ask short questions to track Michael's progress to where Rob Whedbee lay sleeping.

"And you were there. And according to you, you have absolutely no intention of doing anything. Is that right?"

"No, that is not right."

Crabtree's voice boomed across the courtroom, "Well, what were you going to do to Rob Whedbee?"

"I was not going to do anything to him at that point."

"Then why were you in his bedroom with a knife?"

There was a little of that deer in the headlights look in Michael's eyes as he took a long pause before he answered, and there it came, "I thought I had to *protect Lisa.*"

"Did you see anything to protect her from?"

"No."

"But you walked all the way across the room to the far wall from the door with the knife, right?"

"Yes, sir, and when I saw Mr. Whedbee, I stopped, and I turned around, and I tried to leave."

"And he stopped you from leaving his bedroom in the middle of the night when you are armed with a knife. Is that what you say happened?"

"Yes, sir. That is what happened."

"So you never intended to hurt Mr. Whedbee at all, did you?"

"Not after I saw him. No, I didn't."

"You never intended to go in there and kill that man, did you?"

"No, sir, I never wanted to."

"You never *intended* to. Is that what you are saying?"

"I felt like I had to."

Bill Crabtree had Frazier in his crosshairs.

"So did you or didn't you intend to kill him? Which way is it?"

"I intended to *protect Lisa.*"

"Did you or did you not intend to kill Rob Whedbee? I mean, yes or no. Simple question."

During another long pause, Michael visibly rolled his eyes around as if searching for the right answer.

"There was a time when I thought I had to kill Rob, but when the time came, I could not kill Rob."

One thing seemed obvious, Greg Isaacs had prepared Michael not to say anything that would insinuate premeditation or conspiracy and had ingrained concept of renunciation into him.

"There was a time when you thought you had to kill Rob Whedbee. Okay. Let's talk about when that time was. When you were sitting down in the closet to protect the lady you love, did you intend to kill him then?"

"No, sir."

"When you came up the steps with Lisa Whedbee, did you intend to kill him then?"

"No, sir, he wasn't on the steps."

"When you went down the hall, was it your intent to kill him at that time."

"No, sir, it was my intent that, if I had to *protect Lisa*, I would do so however I had to do it. That was what I…yes, sir."

"Isn't it sort of hard to protect someone if you are in the fetal position in a closet in the basement?"

"Yes, sir. It would be."

"She had told you she needed you, and she needed you that night, didn't she?"

"That's what she said."

"Then if she needs you that night, why are you hiding in a closet?"

"So Rob wouldn't see me."

"Why didn't you want Rob to see you?"

"Because I was having an affair with his wife."

"Well, what does that have to do with you going in his bedroom and sticking him with a knife?"

"I had no intention of that at that time."

"The knife was just something you had to have in case there was a potato or something in the closet. Is that right?"

"No, in case there was an attack later."

"But you didn't stay in the closet, did you?"

"No, sir."

"I believe in direct examination you said on June the second of 1994, you and Lisa seriously talked about killing Rob for the first time. Is that correct?"

"I think so, yes."

"So on that date, you and Lisa had a serious discussion about taking the life of her husband?"

"Well, no, sir. She mentioned it for the first time in a way that I thought was serious."

Michael knew admitting that he and Lisa had talked about it would constitute premeditation, and he was trying his best to side-step the quicksand he was already standing in.

"Well, did you talk about it?"

There was another long pause as Michael struggled to figure out how to redirect the questioning.

"No, we didn't really talk about it. I was…"

"She just said, 'I want to kill my husband'?"

"No, no, she didn't say she wanted to kill her husband."

"She said that her husband was going to kill her."

"And she was going to kill him first."

Again, Michael paused and then said, "No, sir, that she had...as he raped her, that she wanted to kill him, but she had not been able to kill him."

"And so she asked you to do it for her. Isn't that what you testified to?"

Michael couldn't remember what he had testified to. Crabtree had found another chink, and even Greg Isaacs couldn't come up with an objection to help Michael.

"No, sir, she did not ask me to do it for her."

"She had thought about killing him, but she told me that she could not do it. She had tried...she had wanted to kill him when he was (allegedly) raping her."

"And so that was all the discussion you and Lisa Whedbee had about killing her husband?"

"On that date. Yes."

"When was the next discussion you and Mrs. Whedbee had about killing her husband?"

"We never talked about killing her husband." *A blatant contradiction of earlier testimony.*

Despite Bill Crabtree's persistent questioning, Michael continued to deny that he and Lisa had talked about killing Rob, but Dr. McCoy's report and testimony specifically discussed Michael and Lisa talking about it as early as April. Michael had admitted to Dr. McCoy that he had agreed to help Lisa by killing Rob. Once again, premeditation and conspiracy were the issues, and it seemed that Michael was still trying to protect Lisa whose trial was scheduled for later that year.

"So are you saying here now that you and Lisa Whedbee never had any discussion at all about you and her killing her husband?"

"Not until...we never had any discussion about the two of us doing anything, no. She asked me at one point if I could kill her husband, if I thought I could kill him. This was after she had, uh, just tried to commit suicide, and we had talked about a suicide pact, and I said I thought I could...I would have tried to kill him."

"You are in the bedroom, and you say you have gone over to where the sleeping Rob Whedbee is laying, and you are standing over him with a knife, and you realize that you can't do it. Can't do what?"

"I couldn't kill him."

"So you did intend to kill him when you were standing over him with the knife."

"That is what I thought I had to do. I didn't want to do it."

Using Greg Isaacs's metaphor about the preacher's kid seeing the light, Michael explained when he saw Rob in the dim light from the window, he realized he couldn't kill him.

"So until you saw him, you wanted to kill him?"

"Up until I saw him, I thought I would have to kill him."

The cross-examination continued as Bill Crabtree asked Michael about his second apartment. Michael responded that the reason for renting it was not for him and Lisa but because his marriage was "collapsing" and he wanted to have a place to live.

Crabtree then brought up the fraudulent 911 call Michael had made from a Weigel's pay phone in May, pretending to be Rob's next-door neighbor. He asked Michael why he drove so far to a pay phone, passing more than four other Weigels, when, as far as he knew, the woman he loved was in danger. Then Bill circled back to the discussions of killing Rob.

"And she had talked about killing him, now, in April, hadn't she?"

"No, not in a serious way…"

"Well, let me ask you this question, sir. How do you talk about killing your spouse in an *unserious* way?"

Bill, ever pacing up and down from the witness box to behind the prosecutor's table, rhythmically back and forth, never let up with his questions.

"Were you as financially secure as Mrs. Whedbee was?"

"No, sir, I wasn't."

"Did you and Mrs. Whedbee ever discuss your future plans?"

"We did early in the relationship."

"What do you mean by early in the relationship?"

"Well, around the fall of, uh, 1993, we talked about the fact that we both felt that we needed to be divorced so the two of us could be together."

"And were you making arrangements to do that?"

"Not at that time, no. That is when we talked about it."

"So even though this woman that you testified you were so in love with that you were willing to hide in a closet on that night and that you were seeing whatever you wanted to see, you never said, 'Divorce your husband and marry me,' did you?"

"Yes, I asked her to get a divorce. I didn't ask her to marry me. I was still married at the time."

"Well, didn't you say, 'Let's both get a divorce and get married. Let's both get a divorce and move to my Brendon Park Apartment'?"

"Yes, we did. We talked about that."

"When was this?"

Michael paused, calculating the months in his head.

"It would have been early in 1994."

"What caused those discussions to stop?"

"When Lisa approached Rob about getting a divorce, he said that he would never let her get a divorce, that he would kill her if she tried to move out. She would leave the house in a body bag."

"When you were talking with Mrs. Whedbee about a divorce, did you talk about her children?"

"Yes, sir. She wanted to be able to keep her children."

"And she wanted to be able to keep her financial security, didn't she?"

"I assume she did. We didn't talk about that."

"And was that part of the reason she didn't want to talk to her husband about divorce?"

"She didn't talk to her husband about divorce."

Michael had once again contradicted himself.

"Did you ever think about why he was doing all these things to her? All these things she was telling you that he was doing, you never gave any thought to it to why he did those things to her?"

"Yes, I gave it a lot of thought. Why would anybody beat somebody up?" Michael offered.

"Why would anyone go in somebody's bedroom with a knife?" Crabtree zinged back at him.

Greg Isaacs did not like the way the questions were going and spoke up.

"Your Honor, is he asking if Mrs. Whedbee gave a reason to her husband to beat her? Is that the question I heard?"

Mr. Crabtree responded, "I am asking if he knows of any reason that Mrs. Whedbee gave her husband to do these things to her."

Michael answered, "There could be no reason for that."

"So we just have a mad man here that beats people up?" Crabtree aggressively asked.

"He beats his wife up," Frazier responded with a bit of his trade-mark sarcasm seeping through.

Crabtree asked Michael why he never went to Rob to intercede on Lisa's behalf, and Michael slipped out another lie.

"No, sir, no. Not by the time…by the time I found out what the abuse was. I mean, I felt that he was just too dangerous."

It was obvious Bill Crabtree was getting increasingly disgusted with the defendant.

"She told you how he had supposedly beaten her, raped her, and caused all these bruises?" *if this was true why had Michael never rushed Lisa to the hospital.*

"Yes, sir. She said it was something she had lived with for years at that time."

"You thought that she lived with that kind of beating and rape for years at that time, but that wasn't dangerous enough?"

"If it wasn't dangerous enough to her, then no. I mean, I didn't think he was dangerous. I thought he was a bully. I thought he was pushing her around, but I didn't think he was dangerous until the first of June."

"And so after May 15, that is when he became so bad that she couldn't handle it anymore?"

"No, after June 1."

Frazier was showing signs of exhaustion as Crabtree tore bigger and bigger holes in his story, and it was beginning to disintegrate. If he so loved and so valued Lisa Whedbee, how could he let her endure constant abuse? If Michael truly believed Lisa's stories of abuse, he had not been doing a very good job of protecting her. Maybe Lisa had made up all the stories to manipulate Michael into killing Rob, or even scarier, Michael and Lisa were working a plan to create a trail of abuse to explain the reason why Michael had to kill Robert Whedbee.

"You talked about killing on June the first?"

"No. The second."

"June the second, you talked about killing?"

Greg Isaacs rose to object and said, "Your Honor, we have already been over this. We are now plowing this ground again."

Judge Baumgartner agreed to keep his ears open, indicating Crabtree could continue.

"Now, June the second, that is when she said she had to do something. Is that right?"

"Yes, sir."

"Did she ever mention that the order of protection went down on the second of June 1994?"

"She said it was dropped."

"No, that order was put down. This order you talked about on direct examination, this order that was going to protect her?"

"Yes, sir."

"You sent her to Sarah Sheppeard. Did she not tell you that that order was signed and agreed on the second of June?"

"She didn't tell me the date, but I knew that it was."

"So this order went down the same day that she decided she can't take it anymore?"

"That is because he threatened her, and he had intimidated her to the point that she was afraid not to drop the order, not to sign the papers or whatever it took."

Michael sounded like he didn't know what he was talking about.

"He, Rob, signed the order."

Michael couldn't hide the surprise in his eyes when he heard that. He stuttered out, "She...it was she that—"

"He signed it."

Crabtree then produced exhibit number 29, the infamous order of protection.

"If you would just read what this says up at the top."

"Agreed order of protection with social contact."

"And what date does it show that this order was entered?"

"The second day of June 1994."

"Thank you."

It had been a long stretch since the cross-examination had begun, and the judge called for a short break after which Assistant District Attorney General Bill Crabtree went back to shredding as much of Michael's story as he could.

"Now, Mr. Frazier, on the seventh of June 1994, how did you get to the Whedbee house?"

"In Lisa's car."

"Earlier in the day, did you buy rubber gloves?"

"Yes, sir."

"And you and Lisa had talked about you going over to her house that night before you bought the rubber gloves?"

"Yes. Before I bought the rubber gloves. Yes, we had talked about my being there."

"What was your purpose in purchasing gloves?"

"I don't know. It was…uh…the whole thing was just so…so much like a soap opera…so crazy and so insane, all I could think about was what do they do on TV. You know, that's—"

"What do they *do* on TV when they do what?"

"Well, what people do when they hide out…when they don't want to be discovered."

"Well, what did you not want to be discovered for?"

"I didn't want to be discovered in the house."

"So the rubber gloves were to keep you from being discovered in the house?"

"Yes, sir. I didn't know what was going to happen in that house."

Michael's lies were sounding more and more pathetic.

Crabtree jabbed and said, "Well, did the rubber gloves give you some kind of cloak of invisibility? How would a pair of gloves keep you from being discovered in the house?"

Michael explained that the gloves made no sense, and because he had been in the house many times, his fingerprints were already there. Michael, of course, would never say it, but he knew damn well what the gloves were for—to prevent him from leaving fingerprints on a weapon.

This was no "fly by the seat of your pants" operation. Michael and Lisa both knew exactly what would happen that night.

"You thought the police were going to go dusting around the house to see if your fingerprints were there, didn't you?"

"I thought they might."

"And you thought they might because you thought Rob Whedbee was going to be dead, didn't you?"

"I didn't know if he would or not."

"But it was certainly your intention?"

"It was a possibility."

"And if he was going to be dead, it was going to be at your hand?"

"I hoped not, and I'm glad it wasn't."

"So the gloves did have a purpose then, didn't they?"

"Yes, sir."

"And that purpose was to hide your identity after you killed him?"

"I didn't know I was going to kill him, and I didn't kill him."

"You didn't go into his bedroom?"

"I went into his bedroom, and I tried to get out of his bedroom."

"With a knife?"

"With a knife."

Crabtree then placed a knife in front of Michael.

"Did it look like this?"

"No, sir."

"It doesn't look like that one. Try this one."

Crabtree actually tossed another knife onto the witness box. As it hits the table, the clatter of the knife echoed through the silence of the courtroom.

"Did it look like that one?"

"No, sir."

"Well, what happened to the knife?"

"I don't know what happened to the knife."

"Well, we know you had it when you went into the bedroom. You had it in your hand?"

"Yes, sir."

"We know that when you went over to the bed, you had it in your hand?"

"Yes, sir. When I was beside the bed, I had it in my hand."

"And we know when you encountered Rob Whedbee, however it may be, you had the knife in your hand?"

"Yes, sir."

"I think in your testimony, you at least slashed him on the ear. So you had the knife then, right?"

"I had the knife. Yes, I had the knife in the bedroom."

Crabtree turned back to the gloves, asking Michael if he wore them the entire time he was in the closet. To his disbelief, Michael told him he had worn the gloves ever since he purchased them around five o'clock.

"You wore a pair of gloves for twelve hours and never took them off?"

"No. It was…I…I was…I was just…I wasn't thinking clearly. I just put the gloves on."

"You put them on and just drove off in your car?"

"I put them on in the car, yes."

"Where did you go?"

"I went home after that…to Jenny Cook."

"Jenny Cook. Was your wife there?"

"No, sir."

Michael's wife, Tracy Doty, had been out of town. Michael had told her he would be attending a meeting that night. When she came home the next day, she found an empty champagne bottle in the trash that had not been there when she left. Had Michael and Lisa been toasting to the success of their plan, or maybe Michael just needed a little liquid courage for what lay ahead of him?

"So you sat around your house with rubber gloves on?"

"Yes, sir."

"So you never thought logically this day until you are standing over this man in the bed with a knife? Is that the first logical thought you had?

"It may have been. It was the most important one."

"Now, we're back in the bedroom, and you are struggling with Rob Whedbee on the floor, and he is on top of you, and you say you just give up and lay there, right?"

"Did you say, 'Hey, I quit'?"

"No, I didn't say anything."

"You never said a word?"

"No."

"Who had the knife?"

"I had the knife."

"Were you protecting yourself with it?"

"No, sir. I never moved it. He was in control. I was not struggling. There was no fight.

"Did you see Lisa Whedbee come into the bedroom?"

"Yes, I did."

"Did she have a ball bat?"

"She had a…yes, she had a bat."

"You were afraid…afraid for your life?"

"Yes."

"Did you say, 'Lisa, help me'?"

"No, sir."

"Did you say, 'Do it. Do it now'?"

"No, sir. I did not. I didn't say a word."

"Never said any of this?"

"Nothing."

"You are just lying there, waiting for this monster to crush you to death, right there, and you don't say one word to stop it?"

Defensiveness slipped into Michael's tone as he answered, "I didn't say anything, and I didn't do anything. I was…I gave up. I did not fight. I did not struggle. I gave up."

"Nothing. Nothing. Well, Rob Whedbee got up off you in the floor of his bedroom next to his bed and ran for the door, didn't he?"

"Yes."

"What did Lisa do when he went out the door?"

"She came over to me, helped me up, and told me I needed to get out."

"Did you hear Rob run down the hall when you went out?"

"No, sir."

"You weren't running right behind him?"

"No, sir, I was not."

"And it just so happened that you ran through the door that Rob Whedbee went through trying to get away from you?"

"That was the door I had come in. I was looking for a way out."

"You are looking for a way out. So you ran all the way through the house, knowing Rob Whedbee is out there somewhere, this monster who is going to crush you. Did it surprise you that he ran off if he had so much control over you?"

"Yes, I was very surprised. I was surprised I wasn't dead."

Michael denied going out the door into the garage, saying he could see Rob outside beating on the gutters. He claimed he then turned and went out the sliding glass doors in the den, which he had passed earlier. Frazier told Crabtree he thought she took the knife from him, but he knew that she had washed it and put it back in the knife block. The police would later find it and evidence of Rob's blood on it.

"And then you ran off the deck and down into the woods?"

"Yes, sir."

"Where did you go from there?"

"I walked home from there."

"How far is that?"

"I don't know. I'd say six miles." (It was nine miles.)

"And then you got home. How long was it before the police came?"

"They were there when I got there."

"So everything that you have testified about happening, as far as the early morning hours of the eighth of June, you really didn't know what was going on? Is that a fair statement? You were just doing what Lisa told you."

"No, I was trying to help Lisa."

"But she was the one directing the activity, wasn't she? Wasn't she the one that you said told you to go down the hall to the bedroom?"

"Yes, she's the one who told me she needed help. She is the one who told me where Rob was."

"But she is the one who directed you into that bedroom and kept you in that closet for that period of time, waiting for him to go to sleep. Is that right?"

"Yes, sir."

Whether Michael knew it or not, Bill Crabtree had once again caught him in another lie—he *was waiting* for Rob to go to sleep.

"So as to whether there was any immediate danger, are you saying Lisa sort of duped you?"

"Not intentionally, no."

"Intentionally or otherwise, do you think she did it?"

"No, sir, I don't. I think she was very scared."

"So you were acting of your own free will, and you were not under the control of Lisa Whedbee?"

"Yes, sir."

"In everything you did?"

"I just wanted to help her. I wanted to take care of her."

"Have you talked to her since this happened?"

"Yes, sir."

"Did you, at any time, ever discuss your testimony to get it straight?"

"No, sir."

"Did you continue to see her on a regular basis after this happened?"

Greg Isaacs immediately objected, the court sustained, and Bill Crabtree ended what he thought was a successful cross-examination. He felt he had skillfully knocked the support beams out from under Michael Frazier's story. He hoped the jury had been paying attention.

Unfortunately, the jury had been paying attention, but they had been more focused on Bill Crabtree's cross examination style. Several of them would later comment that Crabtree had bullied and badgered Frazier to an extreme. Whether or not Michael Frazier was a liar and a would-be murderer, some of the jurors had begun to feel sorry for him.

CHAPTER 48

With the help of AG investigator, Mickey Childress, Bill Crabtree and Jo Helm had gathered a gaggle of rebuttal witnesses. Eleven had gathered outside the courtroom ready to speak to Rob's good character, which had been sorely maligned during the trial. They were eager to testify that none of them had ever seen a single bruise on Lisa Whedbee and that Rob treated Lisa like a "queen." There was no shortage of individuals fully confident that Rob had never abused his wife, much less his children.

Greg Isaacs objected to the number of rebuttal witnesses, and Judge Baumgartner wasn't having any of it either. He restricted the prosecution to three rebuttal witnesses.

Gary Goins took the stand first. A former Knox County officer, Mr. Goins was one of the officers to respond to the Whedbee house on May 15, 1994, the day Lisa had pointed the loaded shotgun at Rob's head. Jo Helm took the lead on direct examination.

Mr. Goins explained Rob had come outside when he and his partner had showed up and had seemed "fairly calm." Rob told the officers he didn't have a problem but that he believed his wife wanted to talk to them."

"Did you go into the home?"

"Yes, we did."

"Did you talk to his wife?"

"Yes, ma'am. When I asked Mrs. Whedbee if she had a problem, she had responded, 'No, not really. We've been arguing.'"

"What did she tell you?"

"At first, as I stated, she said they were just arguing. She also stated that she wanted Mr. Whedbee to leave. We informed her that it was his house too, and we couldn't force him to leave. We explained the domestic violence law to Mrs. Whedbee. After that, she made a statement that Mr. Whedbee had grasped her by the throat, that he had pushed her down, and that he jerked her by the arm."

"As a result of that, did you look for anything?"

"Yes, ma'am, I did. I examined the areas that she mentioned. I saw no signs whatsoever of any bruising, red marks, or any sign that would lead me to believe what she had alleged."

"Is it possible that due to the lighting, you overlooked something you should have seen?"

Goins explained that the lighting in the entryway was not as good as it could have been, but he had used his flashlight to inspect her neck and arms.

"Mrs. Whedbee had hair about to here at that time, didn't she?" Jo Helm asked, motioning to her shoulders.

"Yes, ma'am, she had shoulder-length hair. I asked her to pull up her hair and lift it away from her neck."

"Did she do that?"

"Yes, ma'am."

Mr. Goins said Mr. Whedbee didn't complain about anything at first, but after hearing the domestic violence law and his wife's statement that he had assaulted her, he told the officers that she had pointed a loaded shotgun at him. Rob pulled the shotgun shell out of his pocket to show the officer.

"Was anyone arrested?"

"No, ma'am. I was not able, in my opinion, to determine a probable cause to arrest anyone for domestic violence because I could not find any evidence of assault. I did not witness any assault with a weapon, and there was no way to prove she had assaulted him."

Goins went on to tell Jo Helm that both Rob and Lisa requested that a report not be made because of their children, and at the end, both were saying that nothing really happened, that it was just an argument."

Jo Helm asked Mr. Goins about an older woman arriving before they had left. He did not realize it had been Lisa's mother and could not remember having a conversation with her. But according to Jo Outlaw's testimony, she had immediately noticed Lisa's bent and swollen arm, something Officer Goins had not been able to see because it was not there.

Jo Helm concluded her direct examination, and Greg Isaacs approached the witness for the cross-examination dead set on discrediting his testimony.

"Good morning, Mr. Goins. I am Greg Isaacs. At the time you responded, you weren't a police officer, correct?"

"Sir?"

"You were not a police officer, correct? You were a reserve officer."

"A reserve officer, yes, sir."

"And that is something less than a police officer, correct?"

Greg's line of questioning blatantly pressed the issue of Mr. Goins's capability as an officer of Knox County. He was in for a surprise though when he asked if he had taken any classes on domestic violence.

"Yes, sir, I have," Goins said, smiling at Isaacs.

"What classes have you taken?"

"I have taken classes offered in the in-service training of the Sheriff's Department and also at the Law Enforcement Academy at Walter State College."

"Let's talk about bruises. Mrs. Whedbee had told you this abuse had just happened recently, correct?"

"Yes, sir."

"Isn't it true that it takes some hours and even days before bruises become apparent, correct?"

"I'm not aware of how long it takes for bruises to occur, sir."

"So you can't tell this jury, based on your opinion, as to whether she had been choked, beaten, and hit, correct?"

"In my experience, sir, there are usually red marks present within the time frame that she described."

Isaacs was whipped but went for one more jab at discrediting Mr. Goins.

"What have you used your training to do since you left the force?"

"I am on disability, sir. I have a fractured spine from an automobile accident."

"You are an exterminator, correct?"

"Yes, sir. That is my profession."

"Nothing further."

Jo Helm approached the stand to redirect examination of the witness and asked, "Mr. Goins, did you ask Mrs. Whedbee what the Whedbees were arguing about?"

"Yes, ma'am, I did."

"And what did she tell you, Mr. Goins?"

"She was upset because Mr. Whedbee had permitted the children to go to his mother's house without consulting her."

"And what time were you at the Whedbees' home?"

"I don't recall the exact time," Mr. Goins said, "but it was sometime after 3:00 p.m. when I came on duty."

"All right," Jo Helm continued, "and Mrs. Whedbee was still angry?"

"She appeared to be extremely angry," the witness answered.

"On what physical symptoms are you basing that?"

Mr. Goins paused for a moment and then said, "Well, she was angry to the point she was trembling."

"Thank you very much, Mr. Goins."

"Anything else?" Judge Baumgartner asked.

Greg Isaacs stood and said, "Brief recross, Your Honor."

Isaacs asked the witness, "Now, is it not true that Mr. Whedbee did not mention the shotgun until after you told him that his wife had made a complaint, correct?"

"Both parties were present at the time. Mr. Whedbee was sitting in a chair in the living room. My partner and I were standing in the hallway. Mrs. Whedbee was standing in the hallway to my left."

Isaacs went on to ask about the Knox County Sheriff's Department policy to separate spouses during a domestic violence dispute.

"It is also the policy of the sheriff's department…"

Isaacs interrupted, "Would you please answer my question?"

"Yes, sir."

Jo Helms objected, "Your honor, he needs to let him finish his answer and explain."

Judge Baumgartner motioned for the witness to continue.

"It is also the policy of the Knox County Sheriff's Department, since two officers were injured during a domestic violence call, for partners not to separate to the point where they cannot see each other," Goins finished.

"So is your testimony that you have two policies that are polar opposites and do not make any sense?"

There was a hint of sarcasm in Isaacs's tone.

"They're not polar opposites, sir," Goins defended. "They are for safety reasons, and at the time, we had not determined that there was a domestic problem."

"Let's talk about the real world, Mr. Goins. Isn't it true that if both spouses tell you there has been abuse, it is likely a report is going to be filed, and likely someone is going to be arrested?"

"If there are signs an abuse has occurred, law mandates that an arrest be made."

Reserve officer or not, Mr. Goins knew what he was talking about.

Isaacs continued, "All right then. Mr. Whedbee showed you a shotgun shell and a big gun and said someone had pointed it right between his eyes. You do not think that was probable cause?"

Mr. Goins went on to explain that Rob had not showed him the shotgun and that Mrs. Whedbee had not been in possession of the weapon.

"Therefore, I was not able to determine if she had been in possession of the weapon and had made an assault."

Seeing that he was getting nowhere, Isaacs said, "Nothing further."

The witness was then excused.

Paula Fielder was called next and had known Rob and Lisa for more than fifteen years. She was best friends with Rob's aunt, Martha, and Rob was also her insurance agent.

Bill Crabtree approached the witness box and asked, "Do you know Rob's reputation in the community for truthfulness?"

"Rob's integrity is without question."

"Can he be believed under oath? Would you believe him under oath?"

"Absolutely."

Mrs. Fielder went on to say that she had seen Rob on many occasions at family get-togethers over the years and had a professional relationship with him as her insurance agent. She adamantly said, "He has always been the calmest, nicest, most loving husband and father. I couldn't imagine anyone kinder than him."

"And did you know Lisa Whedbee?"

"Yes."

"Could Lisa be believed under oath?"

Greg Isaacs was quick to object, and Crabtree countered. Finally, Judge Baumgartner allowed the witness to testify.

Crabtree continued, "Are you familiar with her character for truthfulness?"

"Somewhat, yes."

"Could she be believed under oath—Lisa Whedbee?"

"I think Lisa has been unstable for some time."

Greg continued to object, finally necessitating a bench conference regarding the appropriateness of the answer from the witness. After a discussion between the judge, the defense, and the prosecution, Baumgartner instructed the jury to disregard her comment.

"Let's move on here," Crabtree said, resuming his direct. "Did you see Rob and Lisa together?"

"On many occasions, yes."

"How did he treat her?"

"Like a princess."

"What do you mean by that?"

"I have never seen a husband or father more devoted to his family. Rob is very committed to his family and treated Lisa…"

Isaacs again objected, and the judge told the witness to not offer that kind of information.

Undaunted, Mrs. Fielder said, "Okay. I saw them in Gatlinburg at Rob's birthday party once. I saw them in Destin at their condo. I have seen them in my home. I have seen them at Rob's parents and on many times—at funerals, gatherings, Fourth of July picnics in the mountains—on many occasions, and he has always been very attentive and loving with his children and his wife."

"Did you ever see any indication he had abused his wife?"

"Your honor—" Greg once again objected.

"I'm going to allow that," Baumgartner responded.

"Any indication?"

"No," Mrs. Fielder said emphatically. "Absolutely none, and I have been at the beach and in the mountains swimming with them. I've seen her in swimsuits and have never seen any indication of any type of abuse, of any marks on her body."

"Thank you. Your witness."

The defense declined cross-examination, and Paula Fielder was excused.

David Karnes, who had known Rob since childhood, came to the stand and was duly sworn and seated. He echoed the previous witness's testimony that Rob absolutely could be believed under oath.

Having participated in sports with Rob, he stated that Rob was not a hostile person—that he had a cool head, was real laid back, and didn't excite easily.

"Do you know his wife, Lisa?"

"Yes."

"Have you seen him with his wife, Lisa?"

"Uh-huh."

"How did he treat her?"

"Like a queen, to the point my wife would make comments."

"To the point of what?"

"To the point my wife would make a comment about how I didn't treat her like that."

"Hearsay, Your Honor," Mr. Isaacs piped up.

Mr. Karnes answered, "He was very respectful."

"Did you see any indications that he had physically abused her?"

"Absolutely not."

Crabtree concluded his direct, and Greg Isaacs stood up to cross-examine the witness.

"Would it be fair to say that you do not see the Whedbees on a daily or weekly basis, correct?"

"Not daily."

"And is it true that during May and June of this year, you did not observe Lisa Whedbee on a daily basis?"

"That's right."

And that was it for the defenses' cross.

One more character witness was called, but Judge Baumgartner insisted that would be the last.

A small woman in her late sixties made her way to the stand. Reva Patterson had known Rob since he was a very small child, and she added, "When he was in the third and fourth grade, I was the church school superintendent of that department, and I taught him in the third and fourth grade."

"And have you kept up with him as he has grown up and worked and so forth?"

"Yes, sir, I have. The whole family is personal friends, and we do business with the Whedbee Insurance Company."

"And do you know Rob and his reputation in the community?"

"Yes, sir."

"And based upon your opinion and his reputation in the community, do you believe he could be believed under oath?"

"Yes, sir, I do."

"Thank you. Pass this witness."

Isaacs again declined cross-examination.

"All right," Baumgartner said, "we have heard three-character witnesses. Do we have any other form of rebuttal?"

"Based on the court's ruling, I would offer any of these others for cross-examination," Crabtree said in a joking manner.

Greg Isaacs was not amused and retorted, "I do not wish to go out in the hall and cross-examine individuals."

Crabtree pushed just a little harder and said, "I will bring them in here."

"Any other proof?" the judge asked.

"The state would rest in rebuttal, Your Honor."

"Your Honor," Isaacs said, "if we could have until lunch to decide whether we are going to address the prosecution's rebuttal witnesses."

Baumgartner responded, "I can't imagine what that would be on, but I will give you that opportunity."

After five days of proceedings, the end was in sight. Closing arguments would follow the lunch recess, and then the case would go to the jury. Isaacs had lobbied hard for a lesser charge of aggravated assault, but the judge ruled against it based on his interpretation of the law. So the jury would go into deliberations with the option of attempted first, attempted second, and attempted voluntary verdicts.

Rob Whedbee, hoping justice would be served, waited for the verdict in Paul Coleman and Nelwyn Rhodes's office.

The defense and the prosecution had had their say, and both sides seemed to feel reasonably confident with their efforts. It mattered naught. Michael David Frazier's future would soon be in the hands of twelve citizens wearing orange and white University of Tennessee T-shirts.

CHAPTER 49

There was a national spotlight on Knoxville when jury selection had begun in the *Tennessee v. Michael Frazier* case in September of 1995. Potential jurors came in in all shapes and sizes, sexes, colors, and origins—a jury pool comprised of citizens from Anderson, Blount, Campbell, Claiborne, Grainger, Jefferson, Knox, Loudon, Monroe, Morgan, Roane, Scott, Sevier, and Union Counties.

According to the Knox County juror's handbook, not only jury service was considered a duty of citizenship, but also it was considered a privilege. However, many Americans couldn't find an excuse quick enough to avoid jury duty.

On Tuesday, September 13, prosecutors and defense attorneys had chosen twenty-one prospective jurors. Potential jurors had been quizzed about the well-publicized case that had been batted around the media as the "Tennessee Love Triangle." At least five admitted they had read or heard too much about the case to be unbiased. Although Greg Isaacs's motion for a change of venue was denied, jurors would be sequestered once testimony began.

Wednesday morning, a panel of twelve individuals had been selected. Five women and seven men sat on the jury convened to render an impartial verdict in *Tennessee v. Michael Frazier*, and testimony began.

Now, the jury had been sent to deliberate a case that had had its challenges from the onset. For the first time in Tennessee legal history, the media had been granted access to the courtroom. Court TV and local television station, WBIR, had cameras rolling, and print media from all over the country were there to cover the proceedings—enough glare to make almost anyone a bit nervous.

Another first in Tennessee legal history was the use of the affirmative defense of renunciation. Defense attorney Greg Isaacs insisted Michael Frazier had not attempted to murder Rob Whedbee because he voluntarily abandoned the crime before completion. It was a concept the judge, prosecution, and defense argued about throughout the trial, which was said to be "very confusing" by two jurors.

Additionally, the jurors were frequently told to disregard large chunks of testimony or comments made by the witnesses. It's not human nature to unhear something.

Furthermore, the jury did not realize the playing field between the prosecution and defense attorneys was not level. The prosecutors worked with one hand tied behind their backs, forced to walk a narrow path, often unable to introduce the real facts in a case to the jury. Moral responsibility was not always a concern for the defense as they were not held to the same standards the prosecution abided by. In some cases, the defense fabricated scenarios to "aid and abet" the accused.

A substantial amount of bickering went on between the defense and prosecution, and testimony was repeatedly interrupted for what was known as a bench conference—a meeting between the attorneys and the judge at the judge's bench to discuss an issue in the case or an aspect of the proceedings held out of the jurors' hearing.

Technical terminology was another issue for the jury, according to Juror Lemuel Keith who complained that terms, such as malingering, were used without being defined.

Rob Whedbee had always had a blind faith in the legal system. He believed truth would trump lies, and justice would prevail; the innocent would be redeemed, and the guilty would be punished appropriately. Rob was in for another rude awakening.

As the state's star witness, Rob was the first to testify after opening arguments. Because he was a witness, he was prohibited from being in the courtroom except during his own testimony. What he learned about the case came from attorney updates and what he considered to be a slanted media perspective. It was quite unpleasant to read lies about yourself on the front page of the daily paper.

Admittedly nervous, Rob took the stand on Wednesday morning to tell his story before a jury of his peers. He did a good job on the stand, staying calm and focused through direct examination and a brutal cross-examination. Rob was told his level testimony hurt him because he didn't act like a victim. Those who knew Rob knew that wasn't his style. He was well-respected for his honest, straightforward manner.

During his testimony, Rob made several attempts to look at the jury; however, he noticed they seemed to avoid eye contact with him. He had no idea if that even meant anything.

When the defendant came to the stand, it quickly became obvious that Michael Frazier had been well-rehearsed by Greg Isaacs. During direct examination, he continually engaged the jury, almost with an air of congeniality, smiling at them when he told them about his newly born niece.

Frazier didn't fare as well under cross-examination as Bill Crabtree deftly dismembered his testimony. The question to the jury would be whether Crabtree had proven his case beyond a reasonable doubt.

As the week wore on, excitement was growing in Knoxville, and it had nothing to do with the trial wrapping up. The number eight ranked Tennessee Volunteers, led by sophomore quarterback Peyton Manning, were scheduled to play number four ranked Florida Gators in Florida on Saturday night. Judge Baumgartner knew little took precedent over the beloved Vols' football games, which created a concern about the jury's ability to fully focus on deliberation if the trial went into Saturday.

When Friday rolled around, it was confirmed that the trial would go on at least half a day on Saturday, and several options were offered to the jurors including breaking for the game and postponing deliberation until Monday. The jury decided to deliberate on Saturday with the hope of reaching a verdict before kickoff. The judge commended them and, as a concession, approved the wearing of UT garb by the jury in court on Saturday. In the juror's handbook, T-shirts were expressly prohibited in court.

When the jury was ushered into court on Saturday morning, all twelve jurors were decked out in matching white shirts, emblazoned with the recognizable orange logo of their beloved vols. Rob was appalled, and many thought it made a mockery of the system. Later that day, after fifteen witnesses, thirty-one exhibits, and four days of testimony, jury foreman Derek Slayton led his group back to the jury room to begin deliberations.

Right from the start, there was trouble when the first straw ballot was done. Seven voted guilty of second-degree attempted; five women voted to acquit. It would take three more votes to reach a consensus, and so the deliberation began.

One thing both men and women of the jury agreed on was that Lisa Whedbee was the mastermind behind the attempt, and no one believed the abuse charges. Most believed Frazier had been used by a cunning woman who had most likely planned to use the bat on him after he had killed Rob. They all wanted to see her get her due, but the rub was it wasn't Lisa Whedbee's trial. The problem was they couldn't stop talking about Lisa and how Frazier had been manipulated.

Jury member Frank Harvey commented, "You take a girl like that, and she'll get you in trouble."

One of the women said, "As a wife and a mother, I don't think much of her."

Finally, the jury turned to the evidence and went through it methodically, discussing each piece and its relevance to the case. The second vote came out three for second, seven for voluntary manslaughter, and two for acquittal. They still had a way to go. Before the next vote, several jurors wanted to know what the sentences were for each charge, but that information was not allowed.

The jury did not discuss the fact that first- and second-degree attempted require premeditation, which Bill Crabtree had hammered home in his cross-examination of Michael and in his closing remarks. No one had really brought that up during deliberation.

The third vote might have been the verdict, except for one woman who refused to change her vote for acquittal. Derek Slayton was concerned they might have a hung jury, so the eleven members set on attempted voluntary manslaughter began to reason with the one woman holdout.

The jury had been in deliberation for two hours and forty-five minutes when Judge Baumgartner received word a verdict had been reached. The news buzzed throughout the courthouse, and a surge of excited people rushed back to Courtroom IV.

Rob had been waiting for word in Paul Coleman's office when the word came down. Feeling immensely nervous, he made his way back to the courtroom flanked by Paul and his divorce attorney, Nelwyn Rhodes. Rob was hoping for the maximum charge.

When the prosecution and defense were situated, Judge Baumgartner addressed the court.

"Ladies and gentlemen, it is reported we have a verdict in this case. As I routinely tell the audience when a verdict is returned, I do not want any show of emotion, pro or con. I want you to let the jury report their verdict and retire from the courtroom before there is any conversation about it. Are we ready to bring the jury back?"

At 6:09 p.m., the twelve jurors in their out-of-place T-shirts were escorted back into the courtroom, each seeming a little apprehensive about handing out a decision that would change the course of a man's life.

Rob looked at the jurors, trying to read their faces. Michael Frazier sat up straight showing no emotion.

"Very well. Mr. Slayton, I understand that you are foreman of the jury, is that correct?"

"Yes, sir."

"Has the jury reached a verdict in this case?"

"Yes, sir."

Baumgartner asked the jury to stand.

"Mr. Frazier, if you would stand and face the jury."

Turning to the jury, the judge asked, "Mr. Slayton, with respect to the charge of attempt to commit first-degree murder, how does the jury find?"

"Not guilty."

Frazier's face was frozen. Rob's anxiety was high.

"Very well," Baumgartner said. "And to the lesser offense of attempt to commit second-degree murder, how does the jury find?"

"Not guilty."

"And with respect to the charge of attempt to commit voluntary manslaughter, how does the jury find?"

"Guilty."

Rob looked at the jury, trying to understand what he had just heard. Guilty of attempted voluntary manslaughter? What did that mean? He looked at Bill Crabtree, and he suddenly understood. He had been betrayed again.

The jury was dismissed, and the volume level in the court escalated to a roar in seconds. There was rejoicing on the defense's side as Michael Frazier's parents rushed to hug Greg Isaacs and their son.

Although it was a technical win for the prosecution, there was no celebration. Bill Crabtree and Jo Helm gathered their briefcases and motioned for Rob to follow. They walked out of the courthouse with grim faces and did not speak to the media.

When they reached Bill's office, Rob asked, "What happened? What does this mean?"

"Well, I'm never surprised by a jury's verdict, but I did think we'd come out better on this one. Sometimes, they just don't get it. It happens."

"How much time?" Rob asked.

"Four years, maximum sentence."

Rob felt like he'd been kicked in the gut.

"Four years? That man tried to *kill* me. Did they not understand that? I'd be dead if Frazier hadn't been so inept. Were they all idiots? *He said it*. He was going to kill me. It doesn't get any clearer than that."

"I'm sorry, Rob," Bill replied. "But we've still got her to go. We'll get her."

Bill's words were of no consolation. This was not justice served. The unfairness of the verdict stuck in Rob's throat like a large stone. That sense would never quite go away.

Rob Whedbee's life was devastated because of the actions of Michael Frazier. He had been maligned in court and in the media. He had come close to losing his life, which would traumatically affect his life for years. He was now a father to two motherless children, one who required twenty-four seven care and another who was now afraid of strange cars and of his own basement. Rob, himself, would never truly rest easy again.

CHAPTER 50

Long after the trial ended, *Tennessee v. Frazier* made good fodder for discussion and dissection of the case at watercoolers, coffee shops, and by some members of the legal and law enforcement community.

Highly respected attorney Donald Paine slammed the so-called evidence that had been used in the trial in a seemingly comedic piece he wrote for the *Tennessee Bar Journal* in 2005, almost a decade after the trial. In his writing, Paine suggested that Greg Isaacs had presented, in four acts, "the classic hillbilly defense." *The guy deserved killing.* Isaacs's questioning of star witness, Robert Whedbee, was inflammatory.

"Do you admit or deny that you forced your wife to have sex, that you raped her?"

Next question, "Do you admit or deny you told your wife (when she brought up divorce) the only way she would leave your house was in a body bag?"

Although Rob answered that, both questions were "completely false." Isaacs's queries did paint a colorful picture for the jury.

Paine's article went on to criticize the testimony of "shrink" Diane McCoy for all the "double and triple hearsay" she presented as evidence, and the jury, believing it was evidence, got to hear it all.

In an interview in 2013, Attorney Bruce Poston said, "The jury got it wrong. Waiting in a closet for six hours is absolutely premeditation. He defended the legal system, saying, 'It did not fail. The prosecution failed.'"

Poston described "guilty until proven innocent" as a "legal myth, *Alice in Wonderland*."

As far as the renunciation myth, Poston said, "Frazier sat in the closet, ascended the stairs, and raised the knife over Rob's head. There was *no* renunciation."

Former investigator Dan Stewart had really taken the case to heart and was still upset about Lisa Whedbee complaining that her constitutional rights had been violated because she had not been properly Mirandized. He still possessed the taped interview of Mrs. Whedbee on the morning of the attack where she clearly stated she understood her rights and had waived them to talk with Stewart. Dan never doubted that both Lisa Whedbee and Michael Frazier were liars and should have been convicted of all the charges they faced.

Rob Whedbee ran the trial back and forth in his mind and remained disgusted and outraged by its outcome.

CHAPTER 51

Michael Frazier had remained out on bond since his conviction in September, but on November 2, 1995, he appeared in court for his sentencing. Greg Isaacs had used the interim to argue for probation for Frazier, citing he was a first-time offender, and he was suffering mental despair.

Rob had submitted a statement to the judge, requesting that Frazier be given the maximum term in prison.

"Maximum 'actual' jail time, not some halfway house or work-release program. I'm afraid that if Mr. Frazier doesn't get jail time, a very bad message is being sent to would-be killers."

In his statement, Rob wrote that he thought Frazier had benefitted from "a jury who was somewhat less than serious about their responsibility."

Before the sentence was imposed, Judge Richard Baumgartner told Frazier that he accepted the jury's verdict but thought the proof at trial would have justified a conviction for attempted murder.

Addressing the defendant, Baumgartner said, "Mr. Frazier, the jury were very—the only word that comes to mind—is 'kind' to you."

Michael Frazier, looking pale, listened as he was sentenced to four years in prison.

There were many "ifs" following Frazier's sentencing. *If* Frazier had been convicted of attempted first-degree murder, he could have faced a fifteen- to sixty-year sentence. *If* the prosecution had not dropped the conspiracy charge against Frazier, the evidence, as Baumgartner had suggested, supported a conviction. *If* the defense had not been permitted to introduce so much "hearsay" testimony, the jury would not have heard so much about Lisa Whedbee's alleged abuse, and Rob would have escaped the vilification he was subjected to during the trial and in the media. *If* Bill Crabtree had not been so brutal in his cross-examination of Frazier, maybe the jury would not have seen him as a sympathetic character. And *if* so many years ago, Rob had only run…

CHAPTER 52

After the debacle of Michael Frazier's trial, Rob wanted to get away from the legal system, which he felt had failed him. Instead, he had to focus on finalizing his divorce from the woman who had wanted him dead and had orchestrated an attempt on his life. She was fighting him every step of the way. It wasn't the kids she wanted. She said she thought it was best if the kids stayed with Rob—that from a woman who had accused him of throwing his profoundly disabled daughter across a room. Rob knew Lisa wanted money, as much as she could get, and she was squeezing every dime out of Rob that she could. It was a bitter pill to have to pay the woman who tried to kill him. The divorce finalized in November of 1995.

Since Frazier's trial, Lisa had moved to the Raleigh area of North Carolina. After her divorce from Rob, she had remarried.

In April of 1996, attorneys filed notice that they planned to use an expert at her trial to show Lisa had a mental disease or defect when she had allegedly plotted Rob's murder. Her trial was postponed, without reason, until June. Rob still held out hope that Lisa would be held accountable for her crime when her day in court arrived.

Rob Whedbee was in Destin when he got the call from prosecutor Jo Helm. He liked Jo even though he'd been disgusted with the outcome of the Frazier trial. Four years for attempted murder, Rob figured he had to get killed to get justice from the Tennessee legal system.

"Jo Helm, what can I do for you?"

"Hello, Rob. Hope you are well. I hear you and your family are in Florida. You deserve a vacation after everything you've been through."

"So what's up, Jo?"

Jo explained the prosecution team had been in negotiations with Lisa's attorneys, David Eldridge and Tom Dillard.

"We have a plea deal on the table we'd like you to consider."

"You mean no trial?"

"Bill and I think it might be the best way to go. Get this thing ended once and for all."

"What's the deal?" Rob asked.

"She pleads guilty to solicitation to commit second-degree murder for a four-year sentence, one year in jail, three years probation."

"You've got to be kidding me, Jo. That's not even a slap on the wrist. She tried to kill me for God's sake."

"Sorry, Rob. We're just not sure this case is a lock, and we don't want her walking. Think about it, Rob. You've got a couple of days."

"A couple of days? This thing's been hanging in limbo for almost two years, and now I have a couple of days?"

"Sorry, Rob."

Gripped by anger, Rob hung up the phone. He had done everything Bill Crabtree and Jo Helm had asked of him, but he had been waiting a long time to see Lisa on the stand and see her answer for the horrible lies she had told about him. He wanted her to pay for the agony and trauma she had caused his family, especially ten-year-old Justin. He wanted the world to know what a worthless mother she had been and how she had abandoned her children. He wanted vindication.

After talking with his personal attorney, Paul Coleman, Rob was even more conflicted. Paul thought if the prosecution was recommending the plea, they didn't want to go to trial.

"That's not a good sign," Paul advised. "It's up to you. If you want to force the issue, you can get a trial. You just might not win."

Maybe, Rob thought, *it would be better to get it over with.*

A lot of people were telling him to put it to bed and to move forward. It was easy for them to say because they'd never survived or lived with such an ultimate betrayal. He was ready for the fight. He was in the right, and she needed to be outed for her deceit, lies, and murderous plot. He didn't sleep for three nights, agonizing over his decision.

Rob finally gave in. The thoughts of another long drawn out proceeding, and the media frenzy that would accompany it, was too much at the time. He worried that if he forced a trial, Jo and Bill might not get a conviction. He had always been one to finish the fight—win, lose, or draw. And to say he wasn't happy about the deal was more than an understatement. Once again, he felt the legal system was letting him down. Rob felt strongly that not only had the prosecution failed him, they had also failed Dan Stewart, Larry Johnson, Mickey Childress, and all the individuals who had worked so hard to deliver a massive amount of evidence to ensure a conviction on both the conspiracy and attempted first degree murder charges. *It was a travesty*! Thinking about the whole fiasco sickened him.

CHAPTER 53

She walked in the courtroom in her prim and proper blue dress. Her hair was pulled back with a matching bow. Her makeup was meticulous. She was sporting a sparkling two-carat diamond that had come with her new husband. Rob felt sorry for the guy.

On June 26, 1996, just over two years since the attempt on Rob Whedbee's life, Lisa Outlaw (Whedbee) appearing to be fragile, Weatherly spoke in the soft voice, that had once so grated on the nerves of Dan Stewart, and although she had been charged with attempted second-degree murder and conspiracy to commit second-degree murder, she pled guilty to conspiracy to commit second-degree murder, a class C felony. As part of her agreement, she entered an Alford plea, allowing her to assert her innocence while acknowledging that the prosecution had evidence that could convict her. The plea confused Rob, but Jo Helm assured him it was the same thing as pleading guilty.

She received a four-year sentence. All but one year was suspended, and the former Lisa Whedbee served her year in the new $30 million Knox County jail, a far cry from hard time. In her conviction record, Lisa Outlaw Whedbee was deemed "infamous," meaning she would be known for some bad quality or deed—dishonorable and without scruples. *Truer words were never spoken.*

In a sickening moment, Lisa took off her wedding ring and handed it across the gate to her new husband, Keith Weatherly, and mouthed, "I love you."

Rob cringed.

In Lisa's sentencing statement, she said, "I deeply regret that this incident occurred, and I accept my share of the responsibility for it. I am forever grateful that no one was hurt seriously and horrified by the thought that such harm could have so easily occurred. I should not have let Michael Frazier into our house that evening.

"I did not want anyone to be hurt. I acted out of fear, hopelessness, depression, and what I have learned to be a dependent personality disorder. Such that I have always relied upon others to make decisions for me."

Even in her statement, she had to lie. The case against Lisa Whedbee ended with a whimper, and for the rest of his life, Rob would regret not pressing for a trial.

CHAPTER 54

It was Father's Day 2013, and the Whedbee family had gathered at Rob's house to celebrate the dads. Rob looked around the table surrounded by the people he loved most. Four generations of Whedbees sat there—Lloyd, Rob, Justin, and the newest member of the clan, Rob's six-month-old grandson.

Nineteen years had passed since the attempt on Rob's life, and every member of the family had been changed by those events.

Lloyd and Joyce had gladly postponed some of their plans, knowing, full-well, that repairing a fractured family and caring for a child with significant needs could be an arduous task. There was no regret, only the satisfaction that came from being there for those they loved.

Justin, at twenty-six, had been through some extremely hard times, but he moved beyond his own scars. With his father's help, he had put his life back together, passed his insurance exam, and was now giving his dad a run for his money on the commission board at Whedbee Insurance Agency. He was building a good life with a good girl, and together, they had a beautiful son and a nice home. Rob was and is very proud of his son.

Brittany, at twenty-three, still loved watching *Barney and Friends*, forever frozen as a child. She still had frequent seizures and required constant care, but she was a happy girl, loving, and well-loved by all in the family. Rob had always given her the best life possible with no complaints about the sacrifices it had meant for his own life.

The events that had almost cost him his life would forever be ingrained in his being. The unfairness of the outcome still stung.

Neither Michael Frazier nor Lisa Whedbee had ever truly paid for their murder conspiracy, and that remained a fact that would never change. Hopefully, there was a special hell waiting for both.

Rob's experiences had taught him to be more cautious in life. He had been brought up in a world where he trusted people—at least gave them the benefit of the doubt. He was not prepared for the evil he had encountered. Since then, trust had to be earned from Rob. He knew well that not everyone had his best interest at heart.

Rob had learned there are some things in life that just aren't fair and can never be rectified. He had faced death and watched his life go up in a blaze before him. Rob had suffered the devastating betrayal his wife had dealt out to him and their children, but he had made a conscious decision to not live in bitterness or be defined by the events that had occurred. He had overcome much but knew there were some things he would have to live with. He knew he could not control many of the events that happen in life, but he was the one that decided how to react to them.

He found his inspiration in his family, his work, and his duty to care for and protect his daughter, Brittany. Rob still had much to give this world. Despite his sorrows and his regrets, Robert Whedbee's life would go on and, along the way, reveal new reasons for joy.

AFTERWORD

More than two decades have passed since the night Rob Whedbee almost lost his life. Around Knoxville, people still remember the "Tennessee Love Triangle" and the characters surrounding the attempted murder of Rob Whedbee.

Michael David Frazier served his meager four-year sentence and returned home to live with his parents in Kingsport, Tennessee. He went on to become the music director at Holy Trinity Lutheran Church, where he was well-liked by the congregation for his musical talents. On January 15, 2013, at the age of fifty-one, Michael Frazier died. No one knows for sure if he ever stopped loving Lisa Whedbee. In a memorial tribute to Michael, Lisa Whedbee, now Lisa Weatherly, wrote, "You will always be my soul mate. See you in heaven."

As for Lisa, she left Michael (who she would later say she truly loved) behind, remarrying six months before her own trial in 1996. Despite her felony conviction for attempt to commit second-degree murder, she found work with the Independent Insurance Agents of America and later became a human resources consultant with Gallagher and Associates. Lisa made a few brief visits, but even with no legal restrictions and Rob's approval, she has never seen or contacted her children since the 1990s.

Rob's father, Lloyd Whedbee, gracefully surrendered to his long battle with kidney disease, passing away at eighty-two, on July 14, 2015. He is still loved and greatly missed by many, especially his beloved family.

At eighty-five, Joyce Whedbee, even after losing her partner of more than sixty years, is still going strong and maintains her place as the matriarch of the Whedbee family. She is sharp and active, and she still doesn't sugarcoat anything. Joyce provides her constant love and dedicated support to Rob and the kids.

District attorney Bill Crabtree has little to say about the Frazier case. In an interview in 2014, he said the case reminded him of something akin to the Keystone Cops. Rob's determined efforts to get some serious answers from him have garnered little results. Once, Rob caught him off guard in the freezer section of Food City and pressed him for some answers. Bill protested, saying his ice cream was melting, and Rob told him to put it back in the freezer because he wasn't done yet. Their paths have not crossed in the Food City again since then.

Colorful defense attorney Greg Isaacs continues to successfully defend high-profile murder cases. He can often be seen driving his Maserati around Knoxville, most likely wearing no socks.

And Judge Richard Baumgartner faced his own legal battles. He resigned in 2011, pleading guilty to official misconduct for buying pain pills from a felon. He served six months in prison for lying to federal investigators. Baumgartner, seventy, was found unresponsive in his east Knoxville home and died in January of 2018. Despite the scandal, he is still remembered for many positive changes he made in the Tennessee judicial system.

ACKNOWLEDGMENTS

First and foremost, *Rude Awakening* was Robert Whedbee's vision; and without his guidance, his willingness to answer hard questions, and his original journal, this project would have never come to fruition. Rob has become a good friend, and I am grateful to him for the opportunity he entrusted to me. Without him, I'd still be watching the cursor pulse on a blank screen and watching episodes on Investigation Discovery.

Rob and his entire family took me in, gave me full access, and opened many doors to augment my research. I fell in love with Lloyd and Joyce, finding both to be honest, highly intelligent, and caring individuals, who provided a ringside account of what happened. Neither one ever minced words.

My great appreciation goes out to so many who shared their knowledge, insight, and perspectives about the many facets of this case: Detective Dan Stewart; Sheriff Tim Hutchinson; Jonnie Ball; Martha Walker; Suzonne Whedbee; Brian Norris; Hugh Ladd; Joe Anderson; Investigator Mickey Childress; Bill and Suzanne Shinn; Defense Attorney Greg Isaacs; Attorney Bruce Poston; Legal Consultant Neil Cohen; Jurors Paul McKenzie, Roland (Derek) Slayton, Bill McSpadden, Lemuel Keith, Vivian Varner, and Frank Harvey; and also Kyle Hovious at the John C. Hodges Library in the Special Collections wing at UT.

Although taken by cancer in the early part of the 2000s, Mickey Childress's comprehensive investigation reports were a critical part of telling this story, and both Rob and I are indebted to her.

Several individuals asked to remain anonymous, but their contribution to my research was invaluable, and so my gratitude goes out to them as well.

Busy with her own best sellers, Diane Fanning took the time to talk to Rob and give him, and ultimately me, some direction based on her experiences.

Thank you, Andrew Black, the IT specialist who kept my computer and printer running smoothly and taught me a technical thing or two.

A special thanks goes out to former cop, journalist, and successful crime author, David Hunter. He generously gave of his time to provide me with immense help during the writing of this book and became a dear friend and mentor. If you haven't read his work, you should.

Two very smart ladies, Jodi Whedbee and Hannah Sims, spent hours reviewing this manuscript, offering corrections and better wording. Thank you so much!

Many thanks to my husband, Darryl, and to my family and friends, who encouraged and supported me throughout this long process.

To Paul Martines who tried to help me see the person I could become and who is never farther away than a sweet memory.

To Preston Woodruff, Eston Roberts, and Sally Beard who taught me the lessons of literature, composition, and soulful whimsy.

To the only father I ever had, David Thistle Van Covern, who gave me love and taught me my strong work ethic.

And last, but not least, immense gratitude goes to my beloved mother, Betty Van Covern, who always believed in me.

Sheree Ann Martines

ABOUT THE AUTHOR

Sheree Ann Martines

Photo courtesy of Through the Lens Photography.

Fascinated by forensics and true crime, Sheree Ann Martines became intrigued by Robert Whedbee's story after viewing several crime shows and reading articles that featured the attempt on his life. Sensing there was much more to be told, she was driven to uncover the truth and joined forces with Whedbee to bring the project to life.

A prolific writer and a contributor to NPR, Sheree has garnered several awards for her essays, articles, and poetry. She maintains two blogs, which boast more than one hundred thousand followers.

Ms. Martines calls the mountains of North Carolina home.

John Robert Whedbee

Born and bred in Knoxville, Tennessee, Rob Whedbee is a hardworking and successful business owner in the insurance industry. He is known and well-respected in Knoxville, Tennessee, and people, who know Rob, know his word is his bond.

Rob is devoted to his family and the proud father of a son who now works with him and a daughter with profound disabilities whose care is his top priority. He loves his grandkids and spends quality time teaching them about the importance of hard work and honesty and the joys of fishing and sports.

Rob's hope is that his story will inspire others who have been victims of violent crime and betrayal. He is confident that it is "possible to live again, achieve again, and maybe even trust again."